Creating Effective Presentations

Staff Development with Impact

Angela Peery

ROWMAN & LITTLEFIELD EDUCATION

A division of
ROWMAN & LITTLEFIELD PUBLISHERS, INC.
Lanham • New York • Toronto • Plymouth, UK

Published by Rowman & Littlefield Education
A division of Rowman & Littlefield Publishers, Inc.
A wholly owned subsidiary of The Rowman & Littlefield Publishing Group, Inc.
4501 Forbes Boulevard, Suite 200, Lanham, Maryland 20706
http://www.rowmaneducation.com

Estover Road, Plymouth PL6 7PY, United Kingdom

Copyright © 2011 by Angela Peery

All rights reserved. No part of this book may be reproduced in any form or by any electronic or mechanical means, including information storage and retrieval systems, without written permission from the publisher, except by a reviewer who may quote passages in a review.

British Library Cataloguing in Publication Information Available

Library of Congress Cataloging-in-Publication Data

Peery, Angela B., 1964–
 Creating effective presentations : staff development with impact / Angela Peery.
    p.   cm.
 Includes bibliographical references.
 ISBN 978-1-60709-622-1 (cloth : alk. paper) — ISBN 978-1-60709-623-8 (pbk. : alk. paper) — ISBN 978-1-60709-597-2 (electronic)
 1. Teachers—In-service training. 2. Business presentations. 3. Public speaking. I. Title.
 LB1731.P364 2011
 370.71'55—dc22
                                                                                                2010047334

♾™ The paper used in this publication meets the minimum requirements of American National Standard for Information Sciences—Permanence of Paper for Printed Library Materials, ANSI/NISO Z39.48-1992.

Printed in the United States of America

Contents

Chapter 1	It's Not about You!	1
Chapter 2	The Story's the Thing	19
Chapter 3	A Picture Is Worth a Thousand Words	33
Chapter 4	Be Prepared	67
Chapter 5	Practice Makes Perfect	85
Chapter 6	Leave 'Em Asking for More	95
Chapter 7	Good Reads	101
	References	105

CHAPTER ONE

It's Not about You!

The night before giving an important presentation is often a time of high anxiety for the presenter. Handouts must be proofread one last time and then collated properly. Clothing must be chosen and pressed. The presenter needs to rehearse her narration again in sync with the slides, and, doggone it, the remote slide advancer needs batteries!

It's hard not to be focused on oneself the evening before a presentation—and even harder just prior to the presentation as audience members begin to trickle in. However, the first key idea you must internalize in order to give effective presentations is that IT'S NOT ABOUT YOU. Keeping this simple maxim in mind from day one is an important prerequisite to a successful presentation.

Long before the pre-presentation jitters occur, long before the outfit is selected and the briefcase packed, place yourself in the shoes of your attendees. What's important to them? What are their expectations of their time with you? How will the ideas that you're "selling" improve their lives even one iota?

This chapter will help you understand your audience more deeply, apply key concepts of adult learning theory to your presentations, appeal to the strengths and personalities of your audience members, and take definite steps in the planning stages to create presentations that resonate with your attendees.

Knowing Your Audience

In much of the best-selling business literature of the past decade, presentation coaches and presentation designers have addressed the topic of connecting with one's audience, but the advice of several experts applies most directly to staff development for educators. Allow me to recap some of what they have shared that is most pertinent here.

Nancy Duarte (2008), principal of Duarte Designs, one of the largest design firms in Silicon Valley (also recognized as a top-performing, female-owned business), encourages speakers to create written and visual sketches of their audience members—something she calls creating the audience persona (p. 16). The questions she urges presenters to consider include the following:

- What keeps the audience members up at night (their fears or concerns)? How will you display empathy and offer solutions?
- What are you offering that may address their fears and concerns? In other words, how are you going to make their lives better?
- How can you best reach them?
- How might they resist? (see the Audience Needs Map at http://blog.duarte.com/book).

Garr Reynolds (2008), another authority on creating powerful presentations, says that we must slow down in order to best prepare for a presentation, and he reminds us to keep the audience foremost in our minds as we begin:

Busyness kills creativity. . . . people feel rushed, even frantic. So they slap together some slides . . . and head to their presentation. Communication suffers . . . the audience suffers. . . . We owe it to ourselves and to our audience not to waste their time with perfunctory "slideshows from hell." (p. 55)

Reynolds also cautions us to ask questions about our audience and advocates using the questions very early as we first begin planning the content (p. 61). His list of important questions, in part, follows. Notice that the only question about aesthetics appears last, after we consider the people with whom we are supposed to connect:

- Who is the audience?
- What's their background?
- What do they expect of me?
- Why was I asked to speak?
- What do I want them to do?
- What visual medium is most appropriate for this particular situation and audience? (Reynolds, among others, notes that an electronic slide show via PowerPoint is often not even the appropriate form!)

Jerry Weissman (2009), a corporate presentations coach and best-selling author, discusses what he calls audience advocacy in his book *Presenting to Win: The Art of Telling Your Story*. He reminds us that in order "for people to act on anything, they must have a reason to act, and it must be *their* reason, not yours" (p. 7). He says that the key building block for audience advocacy is to constantly ask oneself, "What's in it for *you*?" with the *you* being the audience member (p. 11). He uses the acronym WIIFY (pronounced "wiffy") to help speakers remember this key question and to keep their audience's needs in mind at all times.

Jerry's recommendation is that speakers always find and state their WIIFY before they make any statement about themselves (p. 13). He also recommends the following sentence stems that he calls WIIFY triggers; he urges speakers to use these stems (and others) to make repeated, explicit statements about the audience benefits so that the attendees clearly understand that you are working on their behalf:

- "This is important to you because . . ."
- "What does this mean to you?" (Then explain.)
- "Why am I telling you this?" (Then explain.) (p. 12)

Timothy Koegel (2002), author of *The Exceptional Presenter: A Proven Formula to Open Up! And Own the Room*, suggests these questions for a presenter to ask about their audience prior to delivering a presentation:

- What are their expectations? What needs to be done to meet their expectations?
- What agenda items come before and after my remarks?
- Do the attendees get along? Do they laugh easily?
- Is it a neutral, friendly, or hostile audience?
- What do they know about my topic?
- What do they know about me as a presenter? (p. 106)

In designing and delivering over four hundred presentations in the past five years, I've developed my own way of coming to know my audiences, and in the past two years, I've learned a great deal from the work of Duarte, Reynolds, and other experts cited in this volume. Now, as I assist "train-the-trainer" presenters, instructional coaches, and other staff developers in planning for their upcoming sessions, I urge them to do what I call "audience mapping," a process that borrows from the processes and questions just summarized. The steps I use myself and encourage others to use are as follows:

1. Have a conversation with the person who booked you and/or is facilitating the day (for example, the principal of the school in which you will be presenting to a particular grade level or department team). In this conversation, ensure you understand the facilitator's specific objectives. Also seek to understand any challenges that may affect how you and your material are

received. Ask the person about successes (related to the objectives) that have already been realized; also ask about this person's perceptions of the greatest challenges that lie ahead. If applicable, ask, "If our day together is a success, what do you envision happening six months from now? One year from now? How will teachers have used what they learned?" (You should see connections to both Weissman's and Koegel's advice in these questions.)
2. If possible, have a conversation with someone who will be in the audience (to continue with my previous example, a teacher who will be attending your session). Ask this person what has been communicated thus far about the session. Also (gently) try to determine what pressing questions and concerns might exist for those who will be attending. If feasible, ascertain how this person's perceptions of successes and challenges compare to the perceptions of the facilitator's. If there is some disconnect, be prepared for some discomfort, resistance, or hostility in the session. Plan to address the real concerns of real people—but know that this feat might not be easy!
3. Create an audience map, using both linguistic and visual representations if at all possible. (Tapping into visual imagery will help you connect to your audience in a different way than you are accustomed to; it can deepen your empathy and improve your preparation.) See the action steps and examples of audience mapping at the end of this chapter.
4. On the evening prior to your presentation, review the notes from your conversations and your audience mapping so that you once again feel tightly connected and "in sync" with your audience.
5. About twenty minutes prior to the designated start time of your presentation, stop fiddling with the computer, rearranging chairs, and so forth, and dedicate yourself to greeting people as they enter. Have short conversations with as many people as possible. Remember their names; find out what their specific roles are. In the first few minutes of your talk, state the WIIFY (as Weissman would recommend!) and use examples that highlight the audience members and/or their situations. You will instantly be considered more credible and empathetic. (More specifics about making a good initial impression and about delivering the presentation itself follow in subsequent chapters.)

> ***Self-check:*** *How do I currently learn about my audiences before I arrive to give a presentation? What are some ideas I now have to enact so that I get to know my audiences better?*

How Adults Learn

Principles of adult learning theory (also called andragogy) are significant as you are planning for your presentation. Malcolm Knowles, often cited as the preeminent researcher in adult learning and sometimes known as the "father" of the field, began writing about how adults differ from children in their learning as far back as 1968. Stephen Brookfield and others have greatly expanded the understanding of andragogy in the past twenty years. If you are a staff developer, strive to keep several key premises about adult learning in mind as you plan for your next presentation.

First, adults need to know *why they are learning something*. If the content of your presentation doesn't directly apply to their current situations, you run the risk of turning them off immediately—and turning them off immediately doesn't bode well for you, especially if you have to work with them for an entire six- or seven-hour instructional day or over multiple days.

Allow me to provide examples that illustrate this principle of relevance. Each year as a teacher and administrator, I had to attend a thirty-minute inservice about blood-borne pathogens. (Perhaps you have had to do the same.) Generally teachers would be scheduled to attend this session on a teacher workday preceding the first day of school for students. So, as you might imagine, many of us would be in our rooms, readying them for students, or in curriculum planning meetings with our peers. Inevitably I'd be engrossed in something I considered much more pressing when it was my turn to go to the session, and I was irritated about having to stop the work that I thought was much more relevant (and urgent!) to go to training on this topic that by experience was very rare—and in that particular time of the school year, also quite irrelevant. The blood-borne pathogens session was an example, every year, of a basic "disconnect" with adult learning principles.

Contrast this example with another—a presentation I recently did with several subject-area supervisors of curriculum. They were charged with creating a cohesive, standards-based, teacher-friendly curriculum and assessment framework for a large urban school district. Committees had drafted proposed curriculum in several grade levels in the identified subject areas. However, the curriculum documents were not ready for teacher consumption. The subject-area supervisors had been charged with readying the documents for dissemination within about three months' time. As you may have already inferred, this group was eager to participate, have their questions answered, brainstorm, and basically "roll up their sleeves" and work on the tasks at hand. The information I shared was relevant, timely, and directly aligned with their most pressing needs—the recent directive of their supervisor, the concerns about honoring the work of the committees, and the coming school year, in which teachers would be required to use the curricula from day one.

The adult learning premise of rationale and relevance is most directly related to Nancy Duarte's questions, "What keeps your audience up at night?" and "How can you make their lives better?" If you cannot confidently answer these questions about your material *before* you begin planning the "real-time" presentation (in terms of slides, an agenda, handouts, activities, etc.), then perhaps you should rethink giving the presentation at all!

Chip and Dan Heath (2007) have also directly addressed the need of adult learners to know why they need to learn something or to change their beliefs in their book *Made to Stick: Why Some Ideas Survive and Others Die*. One of the Heaths' core principles is that a presenter should directly appeal to the self-interest of the audience, and they quote successful speech coach Weissman and his concept of WIIFY (p. 179). They fully describe the WIIFY concept in their chapter on the emotional quality of well-crafted messages. The Heaths note that students often ask teachers, "How are we ever going to *use* this?" (p. 179). Obviously this refrain is the student version of the adult's WIIFY, or what I like to call the "who cares, so what?" concept.

Talk to your audience directly and appeal to their needs in as explicit a fashion as possible; for instance, if conducting a session on alternative grading policies, say, "Would *you* like to spend less time grading papers? If you weren't so busy grading papers some evenings, you could probably enjoy a long dinner with your family and even a game of catch with the kids and a walk with the dog!" Look into individuals' eyes and make appeals that will resonate with their emotional needs, not just their rational needs. As the Heaths say,

> How can we make people care about our ideas? . . . Get them to take off their Analytical Hats. . . . Create empathy. . . . Show how our ideas are associated with things that people already care about. . . . Appeal to their identities—not only to the people they are right now but also to the people they would like to be. (p. 203)

Another principle of adult learning is that adults resist situations in which they feel they are compromising their autonomy. They resent the fact that others are attempting to impose their wills upon them (although this is certainly not what you would intend as the presenter!). What we presenters must remember here is that *each audience member's self-concept and efficacy must be respected in the design of the presentation*. Their self-concepts are intimately tied to their experiences, especially their work experiences, and obviously, as a staff developer, you are there primarily to address their work. So by the very nature of the setup, *you may initially be perceived as threatening*.

Adult learners need to feel as if their experience and expertise are being respected; they also need to feel self-directed in their learning. Thus, you must deliberately plan for ways for them "muck around" in your content—to inquire, discuss, challenge, and apply—so that they don't feel that you are holding yourself up as the sole authority in the room or are stripping them of their autonomy. This principle of autonomy is sometimes very difficult to maintain, especially if building or central office administrators operate in a very "top-down" way rather than in a more collaborative mode. Your job is to navigate the situation as best you can and honor what your participants bring to the table in the most respectful ways possible, even if others in the organization are more authoritarian. Your goal is to give them an hour, a half-day, a day, or multiple days of learning that help them grow professionally regardless of their starting points and the interactions they have with others in the system. It's a delicate balance!

A third principle of andragogy that applies to your presentation planning is the fact that adult learners aren't ready to learn something new *unless it addresses an immediate need or problem they are facing*. This principle of immediacy mirrors the principle of rationale and relevance in some respects. Again, you can see the connection to Nancy Duarte's critical questions here: what keeps these folks up at night, and how can you help them address these fears? As Duarte (2008) reminds us, "The audience didn't come to see you; they came to see what you can do for them" (p. 15). You must explicitly and frequently appeal to their concerns throughout your presentation; don't take it for granted that they, who are not well-versed in your specific content, see the same patterns, connections, and implications that you do. State and restate the connections you see, and show them plausible answers to their most pressing challenges throughout the session.

Chip and Dan Heath (2007) discuss readiness to learn, too. They assert that curiosity happens when adults feel a gap in their knowledge (p. 85). If we are to follow their advice, as presenters, we "need to *open* gaps before we *close* them" (p. 85). They highlight the fact that the tendency of a presenter is to tell others the facts—*but the attendees must first realize they need those facts!* Ensure that you take great care to show with your words, tone, posture, gestures, and activities that you have made the participants' needs foremost. Open those knowledge and experience gaps in order to close them!

Make the audience realize (or remember) particular needs that they have, and then show them how the ideas you are offering fill in the holes. Resist the temptation to speak entirely from the "expert" perspective and remember that the people in the audience are really "novices." As the Heaths say, "Novices perceive concrete details as concrete details. Experts perceive concrete details as symbols of patterns and insights that they have learned through years of experience" (p. 114). Just remember that you are not in a room of experts in the content; you are in a room with a wide spectrum of learners, many of whom may be familiar with your ideas at only a surface level. Take care, just as you would with children as your students, to present the advanced information at a level and in ways that help the learners connect with it. The Heaths make an apt comparison between this kind of teaching and chess experts as compared to those still learning the game: the experts "want to talk about chess strategies, not about bishops moving diagonally" (p. 114). Remember that the educators in your audiences want the nuts and bolts—*they need to understand how the bishops move.*

> **Self-check: How could I more explicitly plan for the needs of the adult learner in my next presentation? What do I already do that needs to be replicated, and what do I need to consider changing?**

Appeal to the Strengths and Personalities of the Learners

The educators who attend your sessions are diverse: they cover a wide range of ages (including Baby Boomers, Generation X, and Generation Y); their personalities differ (introverts vs. extroverts, emotional vs. rational, etc.); and they vary widely in their individual strengths and learning preferences (some desire a tight structure while some desire more freedom, for example, and some prefer auditory methods to hands-on, tactile methods). While keeping in mind the diversity of your audience, you may also want to consider some generalizations as you plan.

Recent data indicates there are just fewer than four million teachers in the United States, and most of them mirror me—they are middle-aged, non-Hispanic, Caucasian women (see http://nces.ed.gov/pubs2009/2009324.pdf). To be exact, the average public school teacher is 42.3 years old, non-Hispanic, and Caucasian, and has thirteen years of teaching experience (http://nces.ed.gov/pubs2009/2009324.pdf). Only 7 percent of teachers are non-Hispanic/Black and only another 7 percent are Hispanic. Full-time public school teachers spend about fifty-three hours per week on all school-related activities, including about thirty hours per week delivering instruction.

What do I, as a presenter, make of these statistics? If I'm not told otherwise prior to any given presentation, I can generalize that if I have a large audience, I will see a high number of middle-aged women who are veteran teachers. I might think they have some concerns similar to mine, perhaps—like balancing work and family, since they spend so much time per week on school activities. I may also infer that they have had a number of successes and challenges in their teaching careers and can assume that they have tips to share with other, less experienced teachers who may also attend the session.

A body of research that helps us understand some of the major concerns of teachers does exist. The MetLife Foundation, created in 1976 by MetLife with the goal of helping "people to lead healthy, productive lives and strengthen communities" (see http://www.metlife.com/about/corporate-profile/citizenship/metlife-foundation/index.html), has been conducting the MetLife Survey of the American Teacher annually since 1984. This survey explores teacher's opinions on a range of topics, including job satisfaction. In the 2008 survey, teachers report less concern about class size than in the past (p. 16). They are also less concerned about school violence and feel more confident in their capacity to address it than in the past (p. 17). Standardized testing has become more pervasive in the last decade, but teachers now place less value on such tests than in past surveys. In 1984, 61 percent of teachers were in favor of standardized tests to measure student achievement; today only 48 percent of teachers agree that standardized tests are effective in helping them to track student performance (p. 27).

These particular findings remind me to honor the work of teachers with large classes. I understand that they may feel more competent with large classes than in the past, but they also need to know that I *understand* and *empathize* with the fact that having large numbers of students for whom to be responsible is an ongoing challenge. I also need to acknowledge the fact that school violence exists but also *compliment* teachers on the positive actions they take to ensure that it impacts instruction as little as possible. As for standardized testing, I need to make clear that I *identify with* their concerns about standardized testing and help them see how they make use of the information provided from those tests, plus how they get a richer understanding of student learning from their classroom assessment techniques. I'm always reminded of this old adage as I think through these findings: "They don't care how much you know until they know how much you care." Trying to place myself firmly in the minds of my participants before planning a presentation begins with my *caring* about them and their concerns.

The MetLife survey also illustrates how new teachers may differ from their more experienced colleagues in some respects. Since 1990, the surveys have traced the experiences of new teachers from the time they leave college through their second year of teaching. In the conclusion of the survey authors, "the portrait was one of declining optimism and enthusiasm for teaching" (p. 13). Before they begin to teach, 83 percent agree strongly that they can make a difference in the lives of their students, but after the second year of teaching, only 71 percent agree (p. 13). When beginning their classroom careers, 28 percent agreed that many children come to school with so many problems that it's difficult for them to be good students, and after two years, almost twice as many (50 percent) agree. A fifth of the new teachers (19 percent) report they were very or fairly likely to leave the profession in five years, with significantly greater discouragement for teachers in high schools, urban schools, and schools with large numbers of minority and low-income students. The reasons cited for leaving included lack of parental support (40 percent), pay (29 percent), lack of support from the school administration (29 percent), and social problems faced by students (25 percent) (p. 13).

After studying this information from MetLife, what might I make of it as I prepare to address an audience that includes a number of new teachers? First, I would hone in on the fact that they may feel very frustrated with their sense of "making a difference." Showing them new ways to deal with the problems the students bring with them might help these novice teachers feel more effective, and if they could feel more effective, they might be more likely to stay in the profession. I certainly cannot impact the lack of parental or administrative support or the inadequate pay (and I would argue that the teachers' influence is also limited in those areas)—but I can, as a presenter, help them minimize their concerns in those areas by focusing on an area they are very much in control of: their actions as teachers.

Tammy Erickson's blog at http://blogs.hbr.org/erickson and various articles in the *Harvard Business Review* over the past three years have taught me much about generational differences in the workplace. I've used these readings to inform my practice and share the following generalizations with you in hopes that you, too, will find a few nuggets that will help you during professional learning sessions that you orchestrate.

The Baby Boomers are the generational group that is most well-known and is one that you may very well be part of (as I am). Generally described as being born between 1946 and 1964, the Baby Boom generation is now in their forties and fifties and constitutes a major portion of the teaching force. Most are well-established in their careers, although teaching has, for some in this age group, been entered as a second career or after a significant time away from work to raise children.

Overall, Baby Boomers are loyal, dedicated to their work, and somewhat skeptical. Many teachers in this age group have seen innovations come and go and may adopt an attitude of "this, too, shall pass." (This kind of attitude may sometimes prevent them from being openly accepting of ideas you might share in your professional development presentations; beware!) Baby Boomers will assume high levels of responsibility in the organization and are often appreciative of praise. Appealing to their sense of responsibility, eliciting success stories from them, and praising their efforts will help you connect with these learners.

Generation X is comprised of the forty-four to fifty million Americans born between 1965 and 1980. This generation marks the period of population decline after the baby boom and is smaller than both the previous and succeeding generations. Many Gen X workers saw their parents laid off or burned out from hard work during the last recession in the 1980s, and they see the workplace differently than the Boomers. Gen X places a premium on time with family and friends. They are hardworking but value a balance in their lives between life and work. Because of this, they dislike rigid schedules, timelines, and other work requirements. Required staff meetings and inservices annoy them, and thus they may not be the most willing participants in your presentations, at least not initially.

Generation X thrives on diversity, though, and they like challenges and creative input. They are not loyal to a particular workplace, unlike many Boomers, and will switch schools and systems readily if they find a position that is more aligned with their needs. Members of Generation X value freedom and autonomy; they don't place as high a value on "face time" as Boomers, so they may choose not to eat lunch in the teacher workroom or attend optional meetings. In a presentation, don't be surprised if an Xer offers a very unusual answer or seems to challenge your position; this is not considered disrespectful but is intended to move the learning along and to add excitement. Also, consider giving choices in some of your seminar activities as to whether they can be completed independently or cooperatively. Xers enjoy having a choice and may even lose track of time as they work independently. However, the more they are engaged in the work you ask them to do, the higher the chance of application.

Generation Y teachers are just entering the workforce. Generation Y (also known as the Millennials) is the fastest growing segment of today's workforce. These teachers are creative, optimistic, achievement-oriented, and far more tech-savvy than Boomers. They desire creativity in their work; they want to have meaningful careers, not just jobs. They are excellent multi-taskers and prefer to communicate through e-mail and texting over phone calls or face-to-face meetings. This particular propensity can cause misunderstandings with their co-workers and supervisors. They will also frequently multi-task during your presentation. If this will make you uncomfortable, state that up front, and let everyone know there will be breaks during which they can multi-task and reconnect with others electronically; this particular group will appreciate your attention to their needs to do such. This group might also prefer to engage in professional development via webinars or other methods rather than "live" participation. Also consider ways you can embrace their technological expertise and even integrate it into your session; they will feel honored and useful.

Remember that Boomers and Xers are planners and schedulers, but Ys are not; they prefer looser schedules and a coordination of activities rather than set, linear ways. Ys like to learn as they go, and this can sometimes annoy the Boomers and Xers in your group, because the continuous questions of the Ys can make them seem unprepared or inattentive.

12 ～ Chapter One

> ***Self-check: How do I reflect the characteristics of the generation of which I'm a part? What do I need to remember about the other generations as I plan for my next presentation?***

The Myers-Briggs personality typology is familiar to many educators. When the Myers-Briggs psychometric questionnaire is administered and scored, the person being assessed can make inferences about his or ways of perceiving and interacting in the world. The assessment, called the Myers-Briggs Type Indicator or MBTI, is based on the work of psychologist Carl Jung and has been widely used for over four decades.

Basically, the MBTI presents four dichotomies to its users and asks them to indicate their preferences in each domain. The dichotomous pairs are as follows: introversion vs. extroversion; sensing vs. intuition; thinking vs. feeling; and judging vs. perceiving. Below, I'll summarize each pair briefly and connect to how we might consider these preferences in staff development situations.

Extroversion (spelled "extraversion" on the MBTI) is paired with its opposite, introversion. In the MBTI, these terms have specific meaning that may differ slightly from the general meaning, but in this particular domain, the meanings are very close to the definitions that most of us who aren't psychologists would know. Basically, those who prefer extroversion draw energy from action (doing something) and from interacting with others; they can lose energy and become unmotivated if these preferences are not met. Those who prefer introversion prefer reflection and solitude over action and interaction. Introverts need quiet time and reflective activities in order to rebuild energy. And of course, there are the folks who are balanced in these preferences, and they will function just fine in your sessions if you provide a mixture of quiet, reflective activities and high-energy, interpersonal ones.

Sensing and intuition, which represent the second letter of each four-letter type, are about the ways people gather and understand information. Individuals who are higher in S (sensing) prefer information that is concrete and gathered through the five senses. They often distrust hunches or feelings that seem to come from nowhere; they like facts and details. Those higher in N (intuition), on the other hand, trust information that is more abstract. They trust hunches, feelings, or doubts that creep up from their unconscious.

Thinking and feeling are decision-making functions. Those who prefer thinking are highly reasonable and logical. They look for causes and effects and conclusions that come from a given set of rules. Those who prefer feeling make decisions by associating or empathizing, weighing situations to achieve the harmony, consensus, and/or fit. They consider people's needs first and foremost, while those who are higher in T (thinking) consider the data first and foremost.

The last two letters in anyone's Myers-Briggs type, J or P, represent how we prefer to make sense of the outside world and organize our inner world (our thoughts). The preference represents the way one interacts with the outside world. Those stronger in J (judging) prefer to have a plan—to act after a plan is in place, to focus on tasks, to meet deadlines, and to use routines to manage their lives. Those stronger in P (perceiving) prefer to act without a plan or "on the fly." They mix work and play well and work best right before a deadline. They also prefer to avoid stringent time commitments that might interfere with their flexibility.

The Myers-Briggs typologies may help us understand the strengths and preferences of others who are in our professional development sessions. My own type has been ESTJ for about twenty years; I'm very solidly in the E, T, and J categories, and am somewhat more balanced in S (sensing) vs. N (intuition). One thing I keep in mind as I'm planning workshops is the fact that while I'm so extroverted that I gain energy and learn effectively through interacting with others, *not everyone does!* I do recall some years ago learning that the field of education is populated more heavily than the general population with folks like me, the ESTJs. However, I know there are quite a few people in any workshop setting who are more introverted than extroverted; therefore, I plan a mix of quiet, introspective activities, like short stints of reflective writing, in combination with collaborative, talkative activities, like table discussions. Being strong in the J domain (judging), I prefer to work within a tight agenda, announced beforehand, and I like to provide clear directions for each task. Because of my preferences in this domain, I must remember to be open to adjusting an agenda if I find a need to do so (for example, if the attendees return from a lunch break during which there was some kind of emotional event). I also must remember to provide some tasks that have choice in how they are done, instead of my trying to control every variable.

> **Self-check: Do I know what my own preferences are, and if so, how are these preferences influencing the design of my presentations?**

Jason Margolis (2009) offers some advice to teacher-leaders in a perceptive *Educational Leadership* article, and this advice is appropriate to consider as we close this chapter. He recommends that we maintain a relaxed atmosphere for adult learning and use humor to do so. He also recommends that when leading an activity, we limit direct instruction to no more than fifteen minutes and then allow the attendees to practice, discuss, or apply. He notes that it is also important to build on the work teachers are already doing—ask them to share their techniques and comments, validate their efforts, and then find ways to suggest how they can build on these actions. Avoid talking too much; this recommendation mirrors the advice of Jim Knight (2002), who says that in a professional learning meeting, the presenter should strive to speak less than 60 percent of the time (p. 17).

As we end our discussion of the importance of seeking to deeply understand your audience, I'm reminded of one of my favorite quotations from the book *To Kill a Mockingbird*, when Atticus gives one of his famous little "life lessons" to his daughter Scout. Atticus says, "If you can learn a simple trick Scout, you'll get along a lot better with all kinds of folks. You never understand a person until you consider things from his point of view . . . until you climb into his skin and walk around in it" (Lee, 1960, p. 30). Trying to walk around in the skin of your participants, both before and during your presentation, will enhance your presentations perhaps more than any other piece of advice you will find in this book.

Action Steps: Audience Mapping

There are several ways to map your audience as you begin planning for your presentation. Examples of each type listed appear after the list of types.

1. *Linguistic*: In this method, you can answer specific questions, free write, and/or associate, using words, sentences, and phrases. I've provided samples, in tables 1.1 and 1.2, which show some questions that I'm required to answer in my position as a senior associate with The Leadership and Learning Center, a consulting organization. Consider how you could adapt some of the questions to your needs.
2. *Visual, concept map*: Place a sketch or image of the typical audience member in a center circle or bubble. Then brainstorm around this image. Figure 1.1 represents some work I did as I prepared a six-hour initial training for instructional coaches in the Elkhart Community Schools, Elkhart, Indiana.
3. *Visual, sketch of person*: Sketch a person (a stick figure is fine), as shown in figure 1.2. The head of the figure represents logic (the reasons they are attending) + heart/torso area (emotions, fears, concerns, likes and dislikes) + hands (describe their work) + feet (describe what would make them get up and walk out).

Example 1: Linguistic

Consultant	Angela Peery
Client	Somewhere School District
Contact	George Brown, Chair of the Board of Education
Contact's e-mail address	Georgeisanimportantperson@hotmail.com
Contact's phone number including an emergency contact number (Cell phone)	555-867-5301
Date and time of engagement	October 22–23, 2009
Primary goals	To encourage increased collaboration and data analysis. To increase the use of nonfiction writing across the curriculum as a formative assessment tool.
Description	Day 1, Keynote on Collaboration, repeated three times with about four hundred participants in each session. Day 2, two ninety-minute sessions on writing.
Objectives, if different from above	Same as above. High interactivity is desired.
Audience (i.e. Superintendents, Central Office Administration)	All system employees (about 1500). This is the first time the entire system has come together to have a day of "live" professional learning. Anything I can do to enhance the feeling of community would be good.
Number of participants	In keynotes, 300–400 each session. On day 2, about 100 per session.
Location	XYZ School District Auditorium and XYZ High School/classrooms
Nearest airport	Local Airport XYZ
Drive time	About 45 mins. to hotel

	Site Information
What are the immediate needs of the participants?	1. To understand how collaboration based on data analysis can help them meet students' needs better. 2. To learn a model for effective collaboration so that time that has been provided will not be squandered. 3. To increase critical thinking through the use of writing across the curriculum; to learn or review specific strategies for integrating writing.
How will participants be held accountable for the new knowledge gained?	The system leaders will orchestrate follow-up via staff meetings, webinars, and videoconferences throughout the remainder of the school year.
What are the issues that are most important to this audience?	Successes: Collaborative teams are in place in some schools. This new Board of Education has provided high-quality professional development, including sessions from respected leaders in the field, like Mike Schmoker and Doug Reeves. There is a need to continue to do what they are doing and take it to the next level of effectiveness. Challenges: Some campuses are very isolated and have as few as three teachers total. I need to provide multiple ways of adapting the strategies and ideas I present so that every teacher and every school can see where they "fit in" and can apply what I'm recommending.

16 ～ Chapter One

Example 2: Visual, Concept Map

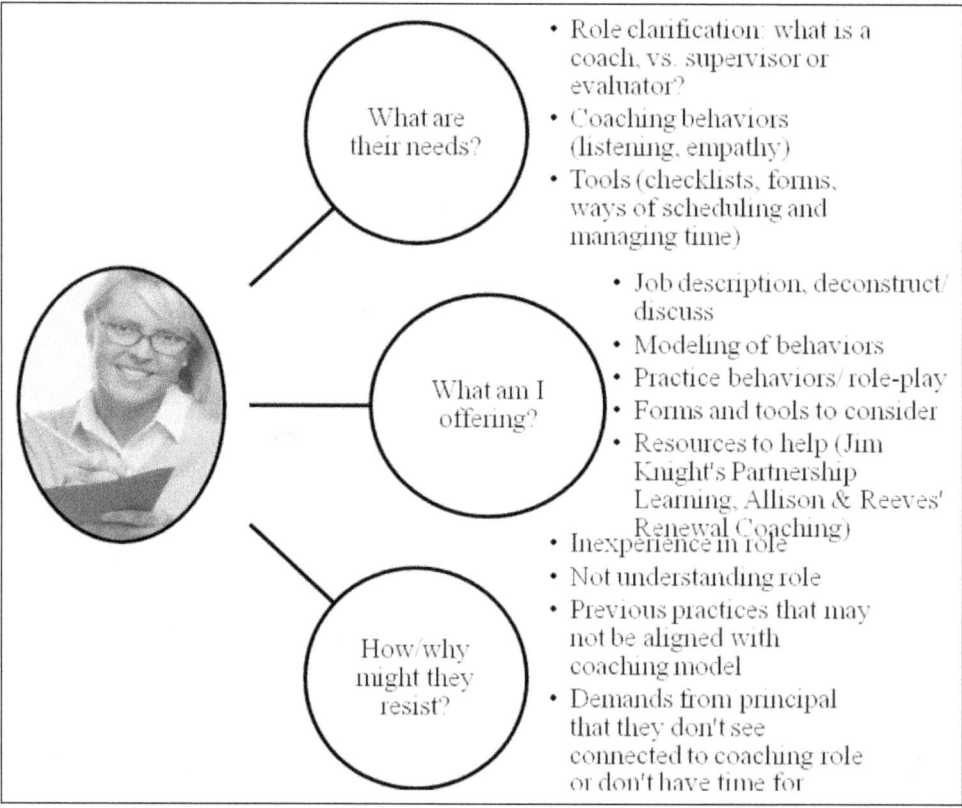

Figure 1.1. Brainstorming Completed prior to Working with a Group of Twenty-five Instructional Coaches

Example 3: Visual, Sketch of a Person

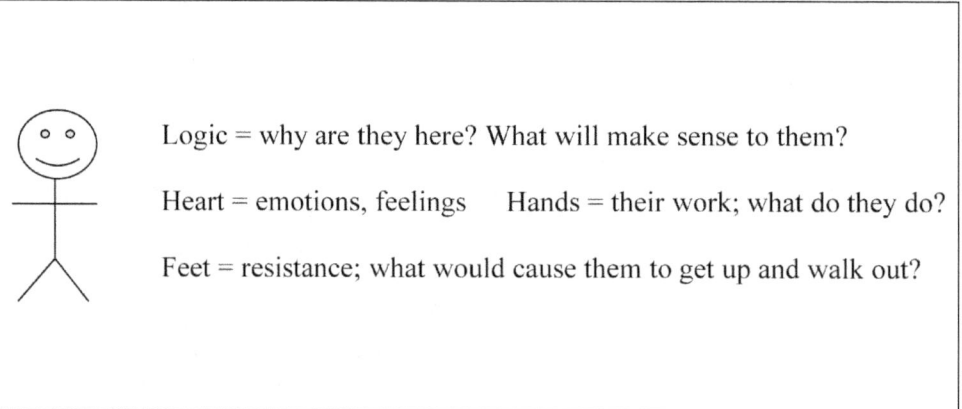

Figure 1.2. Sketch of a Person

Adult Learning Considerations

Record your responses to the following questions and prompts, both linguistically and visually if you desire, in the space provided.

Why do the participants need to know about what I will be sharing? How is it relevant to their situations?

What possible benefits am I offering? *How* will using any of my ideas help them in their work?

How will I respect the autonomy of the learners in my session? What will I say and do to make it clear that I honor their experience, expertise, and self-direction?

Connecting with the Strengths and Personalities of the Learners

Record your responses to the following questions and prompts, both linguistically and visually if you desire, in the space provided.

What will I do to connect with the experiences of *veteran teachers*?

What will I do to connect with the experiences of *new teachers*?

How will I incorporate activities that appeal to both *introverts* and *extroverts*?

How will I appeal to those who prefer to take in information and make decisions through *logic, facts, and their senses*? How will I appeal to those who prefer to take in information and make decisions through *empathy, feeling, intuition, and consensus building*?

How will I communicate the *goals and objectives* for the day while also making it clear that we can *adapt* if needs arise?

Plan for Moving Forward

Review your notes, sketches, etc. Note below your "top three" reminders to carry forward as you begin to craft the content you will actually present. For example, when I reviewed the notes I had made to prepare me for beginning my work with the instructional coaches in Elkhart, Indiana (see above), I noted these as my top three:

1. Define and clarify what a coach does vs. an evaluator, mentor, or supervisor.
2. Build on what they have already done and allow them to share their successes, tips, etc.—building trust so that they will also share their questions and concerns fearlessly.
3. Give them practical tools they can use immediately, like a post-observation feedback form to use with teachers with whom they are working.

List your top three.

CHAPTER TWO

~

The Story's the Thing

In the earliest moments after you've been asked to lead a professional development session, what are you thinking? If a vision of PowerPoint dances through your head, you, like millions of other frequent presenters, have misplaced your priorities. You have fallen under the spell of the captivating and easy-to-use Microsoft product!

Your initial thoughts should be about your compelling story, your chief message, the key points you will drive home—not about designing the visual backdrop (that is, the PowerPoint slides). The skillful crafting of your story should come long before you ever touch the keyboard.

This chapter will give you suggestions for creating the big idea, for emphasizing the most important points that allow your attendees to really "get" the big idea, and for planning for visual and emotional impact through storyboarding.

What's the Big Idea?

In teaching educators all over the country how to better understand the standards they are required to teach, I often share the work of my colleague Larry Ainsworth. Larry and the rest of us at The Leadership and Learning Center advocate a process called "unwrapping" the standards, and part of this process includes developing essential questions and big ideas to help both teachers and students connect the standards to interdisciplinary understanding and lifelong learning.

In our "Unwrapping" the Standards seminar, we explain what a big idea is by saying that it's what you want your students to discover *on their own* as a result of instruction. In other words, it's the "a-ha" realization that students have when they have learned something important (The Leadership and Learning Center, 2009, Engaging Classroom Assessments seminar).

A big idea for any presentation a staff developer might give is really no different. It's the one thing, stated succinctly, that you want your audience to deeply understand, the one thing that calls them to action.

Garr Reynolds (2008) echoes this concept beautifully when he says, "If the audience could remember only one thing (and you'll be lucky if they do), what would you want it to be?" (p. 61). Thinking and writing in response to that simple but provocative question will bring you clarity as you begin to plan your presentation.

Doug Neff, who works with Nancy Duarte, focused on the concept of the big idea in one of the articles on the Duarte site (http://blog.duarte.com/2009/01/did-you). There he calls the big idea "the essence of your presentation, the reason you brought it into being, the moral of your story, your thesis statement, your brass ring . . ."

Neff says, "If you're not sure yet what your big idea is, drop what you're doing and figure it out" (http://blog.duarte.com/2009/01/did-you). Stating your big idea is the one thing you must do before you do anything at a computer keyboard and screen.

Table 2.1 provides some big idea statements for presentations I've given recently. They are offered only to provide context and to trigger possibilities for you. They are not intended to be extraordinary, unique, or even worthy of emulating. Just stating big ideas prior to drafting should help you plan your presentations more deliberately. Consider these statements, and, if so inspired, reflect on a few of your past presentations, and capture the big ideas you communicated in the chart alongside mine.

If that exercise was easy for you, bravo! You already know something about the concept of big ideas and are well on your way to creating future presentations that demonstrate big ideas well and capture the minds and hearts of your audience.

If you struggled with stating the big ideas for presentations you have already given, imagine how the audience felt! You were the person who knew the most about the topic, and if you are still unable to state the big idea succinctly, then the idea was definitely not clear enough.

The action steps at the end of this chapter will assist you in articulating and clarifying your big ideas for upcoming presentations.

> ***Self-check:*** *Record words, phrases, sentences, and/or images that represent the one big idea you want your audience to remember from an upcoming presentation. Write and sketch until you feel comfortable that your representation accurately reflects the most important content and implies the call to action you will make.*

My Big Idea Statement	Your Big Idea Statement
PowerPoint presentations are often not the best "co-teachers" of content that is presented to educators. Audience: National Staff Development Council annual meeting, Dec. 2009.	
Teachers' grading policies are often idiosyncratic, unrelated to overall academic achievement, and punitive; if we don't change how we grade, we are doing a terrible disservice to students. Audience: Lakeland Public Schools, New York, Nov. 2009.	
Webinars can be effective learning tools if well-constructed and engaging. Audience: Colleagues at The Leadership and Learning Center, Fall Retreat, Nov. 2009.	
Collaborative teams of teachers can address identified student needs better than individual teachers can, and high-quality, common assessments are the key. Audience: Warren Harding High School, Bridgeport, CT, Nov. 2009.	
When we increase the amount of writing students do in our classes, we deepen understanding, regardless of the content area or course in which we are teaching. Audience: Teachers at Sir Robert Borden Junior High, Dartmouth, Nova Scotia, Canada, Nov. 2009.	
Effective instructional coaching involves trust and a great deal of relationship building in addition to content knowledge. Audience: Instructional coaches, Elkhart Community Schools, Elkhart, IN, Nov. 2009.	

Crafting the Story with the Big Idea in Mind

As small children, the first text structure we all learn is that of the narrative, and more specifically, the fictional narrative. We internalize this structure early if we are fortunate enough to have our parents, siblings, and/or other caretakers reading to us, or later, when we begin attending school.

Remember "Little Red Riding Hood"? In this story, we have a sympathetic character, much like ourselves, perhaps, setting off to do a good thing—visiting her ailing grandma to deliver baked goods. However, she has to travel through the deep, dark forest, and she has been warned by her mother not to go off the established path.

She does veer off, and she then runs into a problem, namely, the wolf. The wolf gets rid of grandma and disguises himself as her. There are various versions of the ending, some more violent than others, but in all of them, Little Red Riding Hood is saved and learns a lesson about whom to trust and how much information about oneself to share with strangers.

This familiar children's story has elements that you should replicate in a presentation. The audience for "Little Red Riding Hood" is impressionable children. A secondary audience is parents who want to teach those same children important lessons. Remember that the audience is of vital importance when planning any presentation. A story audience is not much different.

In the story, the character and setting are established immediately. Child readers readily empathize. They might like to be trusted to go to Grandma's house alone. This task appeals to their sense of increasing independence. They also like to picture themselves as caring and kind. Spending time with an elderly relative would seem to be a very loving thing to do, and children might aspire to this task.

What can "Little Red Riding Hood" teach presenters? Establish a reasonable context and create empathy from the beginning of the presentation. As the Heath brothers (2007) say, get people to take off their analytical hats immediately. Create empathy. Show them how the ideas you're sharing are linked to things they care about. Appeal to the audience's self-interests and identities, and remember that "story is part entertainment and part instruction" (p. 209).

Indeed, the best stories, like "Little Red Riding Hood," endure because they are entertaining yet also provide a life lesson. You want your presentation to do the same—teach something new, be engaging, and leave participants with a lesson learned.

Now back to the story. Red Riding Hood seems to be somewhat like us, if we are reading the story from a child's point of view. She has good intentions, loves her grandmother, and is excited to be able to set off on her own through the woods.

Next, she runs into a problem. She acts in a way that might be how we would act—namely, she disobeys her mother and then finds herself in a tricky situation with the wolf.

Lesson for the presenter: Participants have needs and concerns they want addressed. They may have tried to address them already, but without much success. Help them find at least one way to improve their situation.

What is the best solution? That's what you, the presenter, must offer. Ask, do you spend too much time grading papers? Yes? Then let me provide you with some ways where you can cut that time in half. Or, do you have students who seem unmotivated? Let me share some new ideas to engage them. How about, would you like your students to be more successful in mastering the academic content of your class? Terrific! Let me help you design formative assessment tasks that will help you do just that.

Last, in our story, the problem is resolved. In most modern versions, our pal Red Riding Hood is saved from death, and she articulates the important lesson that she has learned (which varies across story versions). Basically, she sees the error of her ways and promises to act differently in the future.

Lesson for the presenter: Ensure the audience leaves knowing the one big idea you wanted to communicate—the moral of the story, if you will.

Also ensure that the audience members have been able to internalize one strategy for addressing their needs or concerns. They must be able to give a direct answer to the WIIFY. If asked, "What's in it for you?" each person should be able to say, "I can do X, and it will help me because Y." For example, "If I stop scoring homework for correctness, and instead check it only for completeness, I'll save precious time, and students will start to see that the value of homework in my class is in the practice."

In the excellent resource *Beyond Bullet Points*, Cliff Atkinson (2008) advocates the use of a three-part dramatic structure when planning a presentation. Unlike Duarte and Reynolds, who advocate a more free-flowing, creative process, Atkinson presents a series of highly specific steps.

Even though others have disagreed with his format, he advises presenters to use a story structure very similar to the "Little Red Riding Hood" structure I described previously. He calls these sections Acts I, II, and III because of their similarities to movie scripts, which themselves trace their heritage to the structure of Greek storytelling (p. 60).

Atkinson's Act I is the part that persuades your audience to focus on your message. Part of this act is setting up the movement from point A (where the audience is now) to point B (the desired state). You are to state in the beginning of your presentation what points A and B are.

Act II includes the logical reasoning, and Act III presents a call to action. However, it is Act I that sets the emotional tone for the entire presentation, and Atkinson argues that you must do this *within the first five slides*. The objectives of these first few slides are to connect emotionally with the audience, define a problem they face, and present a possible solution (p. 64). No expert would disagree with him that the first five slides are critical. The body of the presentation then enumerates the action steps that align with the solution(s) you propose.

In a bit of contrast to Atkinson, Jerry Weissman (2009) cautions us to "let the right brain complete its stream-of-consciousness cycle *before* applying the left brain's structure. Focus *before* flow" (p. 23). Weissman means that a presenter should draft all possible ideas and connections that emanate from the big idea/core message *before* creating the story sequence. Like Duarte, Reynolds, and others, Weissman urges presenters to be creative and free-flowing before imposing rigid structure. And, just like writing teachers tell their students, prewriting (or in this case, pre-creating) is very important. Without good pre-creating, the story suffers.

Duarte and Reynolds encourage presenters to tap into their childlike, creative sides when beginning to plan a presentation, moving to a crisper, more linear structure later. Neither of them advocates any specific order to the pre-planning. However, both of them also reference Atkinson's work and recommend it. If you are a highly logical, orderly person, and the thought of sketching, talking, and writing about free-flowing ideas makes you uncomfortable, by all means, check out Atkinson's Act I, II, III advice. It may work well for you.

Reynolds (2008) emphasizes the six components of "sticky" ideas as shared by Chip and Dan Heath (2007) as a framework during the creative process. These components are simplicity, unexpectedness, concreteness, credibility, emotions, and stories (p. 77).

These ideas, as applied to the work of professional developers, have some key ideas.

One, as Reynolds notes, "You must be ruthless in your efforts to simplify . . . your message to its absolute core. . . . What's the core? Why does it matter?" (p. 77). You must give real examples, not abstractions, that can be visualized (p. 77).

Success stories of real teachers, real students, and real schools help make your ideas concrete. A presenter I've seen recently tells the story of an improved school system through the eyes of a child who was in elementary school when the major school reforms started. This child later became valedictorian of her class. After presenting the data about the initiatives that the schools undertook, the presenter tells the story of the student, briefly, and then shows an excerpt of the valedictory speech. This emotional touch drives the point home: school improvement efforts impact the lives of real kids. I've seen this presentation several times, and I still get teary-eyed when watching. Imagine how powerful it is on audiences who see it only once.

As for crafting one's story, Reynolds says, "Good stories have interesting, clear beginnings; provocative, engaging content in the middle; and a clear conclusion" (p. 80).

Reynolds does caution us to "show restraint at all times and bring everything back to the core message" (p. 97). Removing extraneous material, including unrelated anecdotes, will strengthen your core. The presentation described above includes one very powerful anecdote that ties all the pieces together. It doesn't wander off-message by including side anecdotes.

I recently heard complaints expressed about a presenter that had worked with a group a few weeks before I showed up. The teachers who had attended said, "I don't remember much about the process he was trying to teach, but I do remember that he has two young sons and he had recently chaperoned a field trip for one of their classes." It seems this particular presenter had included the unrelated anecdote, and while it may have been endearing, it obscured his main point—which was to teach the specific process.

Weissman calls the concept of the big idea or core message the clear point. He also notes that one of the five cardinal sins of presentations is having "no clear point" (2009, p. 1). Have you ever been the victim of the three-hour presentation after which you said, "Gee, what was that about?" If so, the core was obscured. Presenters must avoid this *at all costs*. Sharing stories about one's family, telling jokes, showing unrelated video clips, and "bird-walking" all interfere with the expression of your clear point.

Weissman names his story development stages the following:

- Brainstorming, during which "you'll find that ideas pop up all over the place" (p. 33).
- Clustering, during which you reduce the numerous ideas you generated into five or six "Roman columns," or pillars formed from key points (p. 25).
- Choosing a flow structure (p. 42) after you consider sixteen different ones (p. 43).

Whereas Atkinson's Acts I through III can have any structure you wish, Weissman urges you to choose one or more of the sixteen specific flow structures that best match your information and to consistently emphasize linkages among the key points (represented by the Roman columns). As he says, your audience has access to your content only one slide at a time and "it's like looking at a forest at the level of the trees" (p. 42).

As a presenter, you need to explicitly and repeatedly make the connections among "trees." Do not force your audience members to "glaze over" because you are presenting too many isolated facts. Do not encourage them to interrupt you for clarification, thereby preventing their active listening (p. 42).

Remember that you are the expert here, but you have to present information at a novice's level of abstraction. Take yourself back to the non-expert mind when you craft your slides. Help the big picture come together for your audience, who understands the connections at a level far less nuanced than yours.

Consider the connections among Atkinson's objectives for Act I, Duarte's audience persona questions, Reynolds' guidance about preparing your story, the WIIFY concept as related by the Heath brothers, and idea of the Roman columns and the "tree vs. forest" view presented by Weissman. All these experts urge presenters to do pretty much the same thing—connect, address, and compel.

Personally connect, then address a real need, and last, compel action. Achieving these goals depends heavily on a defined core message and appropriate chunks of information presented in a logical structure and a warm, engaging manner.

> ***Self-check:** What do I need to remember about the topic of my upcoming presentation so that I avoid overloading my audience with too much information or information at too high of a level for their understanding? What connections among subtopics are present but are most likely not clear to the attendees?*

Adding Detail and Context to the Big Idea: The Support

Once you have established your big idea or central message, sketch out the supporting ideas through brainstorming and clustering. Atkinson suggests the three acts, as if you are crafting a dramatic script. Reynolds and Weissman recommend clustering as ideas form and seem connected. Reynolds recommends three to five of these clusters, whereas Weissman allows for as many as six.

Duarte (2008) encourages presenters to sketch their way to success by "taking rough ideas, fine tuning them, reorganizing them, and sketching it out all over again until you can see a story" (p. 32). She also advises presenters to walk another person through their sketches and to see if ideas are further clarified by doing so (p. 34). Her recommendations are much less linear and more collaborative than those of Cliff Atkinson and others.

Reynolds (2008) states, "Presentations are not just about following a formula for transferring facts . . . by reciting a list of points on a slide. (If it were, why not send an e-mail and cancel the presentation?) What people want is something fundamentally more human . . . 'the story' of your facts" (p. 82). His storyboarding process consists of four parts: brainstorming, grouping, storyboarding off the computer, and storyboarding at the computer. Notice that sitting at keyboard and screen come after three other steps have been taken.

Allow me to share a framework that blends the ideas of all these thinkers in a simple way. I call it "thinking like a reporter." As a presenter, you must consciously address the who, what, when, where, why, and how of your core message and its subcomponents, so why not also use these reporter's questions as you prepare?

Let's return to an earlier example and work through the questions. The big idea of one of my recent presentations was "Teachers' grading policies are often idiosyncratic, unrelated to overall academic achievement, and punitive; if we don't change how we grade, we are doing a terrible disservice to students."

You can probably see some of the supporting ideas embedded in the statement: inconsistent policies among teachers, non-academic factors factored into grades, and low grades being used punitively. The call to action was woven throughout the half-day session I led. That call to action was that we (educators) must reflect on how we currently grade and make changes to ensure that grades better reflect student learning and not other variables.

So in this particular presentation, the *who* consisted of the teachers and administrators in my session along with me—together we would explore the topic and its relevance to needs in their system.

The *what* was the evaluation of student work and the grades that result from that evaluation. This particular chunk of learning contained sub-points about forms of assessment, the purposes of feedback and evaluation, and classroom grading policies.

The *when* was the current school year, particularly the second semester, when the central office administrators expected teachers and principals to make changes to existing practice as a result of this session, professional reading, and monthly collaborative meetings. The concept of *when* also included the past, because some individual grading policies had come to light over several years and were difficult for administrators to understand and/or defend.

Where encompassed the entire system, which consists of several elementary schools, one large middle school, two comprehensive high schools, and an alternative high school.

Lastly, *why* should teachers consider changing their grading methods—what were the compelling reasons, the "who cares and so what" or the WIIFY? In this case, the compelling reason was that motivation and learning are enhanced when certain changes are made.

Through a simulation using a student's actual grades from one quarter, I demonstrated how a group of intelligent, reasonable educators could arrive at vastly different report card grades for the student. This activity drove two key sub-points home for the group: that grading is inconsistent from teacher to teacher and that it can also be severely punitive. Another subtopic, that grading sometimes doesn't reflect only academic learning but also behaviors, was addressed with a small-group cooperative learning task. The last component of the presentation was for the audience to figure out *how* they could actually begin the work.

"Thinking like a reporter" helped me consider that presentation from various angles. As I think, write, and sketch through such questions prior to a presentation, I strengthen and clarify not only my core message but also work toward a desired structure, often chunking bits and pieces together as I draft.

The Heath brothers (2007) provide one of the most compelling examples of how chunking information into sensible segments aids learning. This example will close this section.

After reminding us that the compactness of any message enhances its likelihood of "sticking," they present the activity below (p. 51).

Look at the list of letters below for no more than 15 seconds. Try to remember as many of them, in the proper order, as possible.

J FKFB INAT OUP SNA SAI RS

Most people can remember 7–10 letters. Now try it this way. Look at the same letters, regrouped, below.

JFK FBI NATO UPS NASA IRS

Did you remember more this time around? Of course you did! The letters now appear as acronyms that we all identify. This exercise clearly demonstrates the power of chunking information in meaningful, digestible, and relevant groups.

For another example of my own brainstorming and clustering, see figure 2.2 at the end of this chapter. What you'll see is the initial sketching out of my ideas for the book you are now reading. Again, this example is provided to you in the hopes that it triggers your own ideas, not as a specific template you must follow or an "ideal."

> ***Self-check, linguistic method:** Draft ideas in response to the reporter's questions to help determine the subtopics that must be included in your upcoming presentation. List who, what, when, where, why, and how.*

> ***Self-check, visual method:** Sketch the ideas you have for the subtopics of your presentations in the form of Roman columns or in column-like boxes. See, for example, figure 2.1.*

In closing this chapter, let me share with you one of the most interesting findings of the Heath brothers (2007). In the average one-minute speech, the typical public speaking student uses 2.5 statistics. Only one student in ten tells a story. But when audience members (other students) recall the speakers, 63 percent remember the stories. *Only 5 percent remember any statistic that was shared* (p. 243).

The Story's the Thing ~ 29

Figure 2.1. Roman Column Sample

What can we learn from this? Crafting a compelling story that makes use of real examples and emotional connections will help your audience learn and remember.

Action Steps

1. Review your "top three" list from chapter 1. Are there any other questions you need to ask of the facilitator of your next session? Do you still feel your top three reminders are the most important ideas that you want to carry forward as you draft your story?

30 ～ Chapter Two

2. Identify and articulate your big idea. Write several drafts if necessary. Refer to the self-check prompt earlier in this chapter and mold it into a succinct statement that identifies your core message and implies the call to action you will make.
3. Brainstorm the entire story, including all important chunks of information. Refer to the self-check exercises you already completed in this chapter. Represent the complete story below, in words and pictures or in any way that you feel captures it well.
4. Storyboard away from the computer. Nancy Duarte (2008) recommends using one Post-It note per idea, and suggests using a regular-tip Sharpie marker. Why? "If it takes more space than a Post-It and requires more detail than a Sharpie can provide, the idea is too complex" (p. 28). So, using

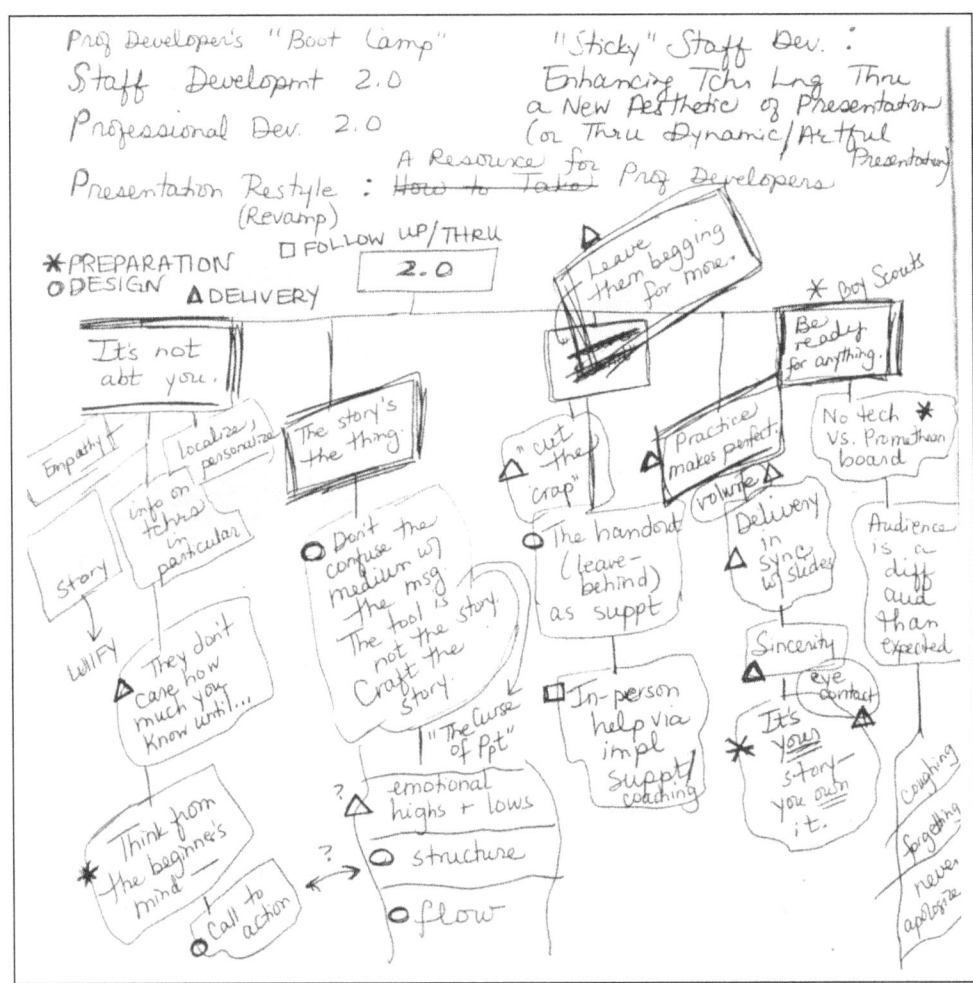

Figure 2.2. Example of Brainstorming and Clustering

Post-It notes, a whiteboard, pen and paper, or any other "non-computer" method, start planning how you will tell your story using slides. Garr Reynolds (2008) offers the idea of printing out blank PowerPoint slides in the handout pattern of three slides per page with lines for notes on the side (p. 87). If you use this format, be sure to sketch *visuals* in the boxes and write words, phrases, and sentences on the lines; force yourself to think in *images* that match your points.
5. Put your storyboards away and let them "cool off" for at least a day. Then take Garr Reynolds' (2008) advice and "edit like crazy" (p. 95). View your entire storyboard and draft everything from the novice's mind, not your own expert mind. Ensure you are emphasizing your core message and are not overloading the working memory of your participants. If you cannot construct a direct line from any given point back to your big idea, *then take that point out*.
6. Ensure your hand-drafted storyboard is understandable. In the next chapter, you will move from storyboarding by hand to storyboarding in PowerPoint.

CHAPTER THREE

∼

A Picture Is Worth a Thousand Words

After you have developed your story, including your one big idea and key points in support of that idea, you're ready to develop the accompanying visual backdrop for your teaching.

One critical aspect of the slide show is the images you use. This chapter will include a section on the effective selection and use of photographic images in your presentations. Other important design elements (backgrounds, fonts and text size, and representations of data) are also addressed.

This chapter is intended to be a starting point for you as you seek to improve the design of presentations you must give; it is not intended to provide in-depth guidance. If you begin tinkering with design as a result of this chapter and then want to become even more design-savvy, the very next book you read should be Garr Reynolds' *Presentation Zen*. If you can read only one book after the one you're reading now, *make it that book!*

If you have the time and energy to commit to reading two books, you should also tackle Nancy Duarte's *Slideology*. You can consider yourself having completed a "mini-course" in slide show design if you study both of these books.

And even if you read nothing else after this chapter, you will be equipped to make significant changes to your presentations that will help them stand out from the norm.

A Brief History of Microsoft PowerPoint

You may be surprised to find out that the PowerPoint program was not invented for teaching. Reportedly, it was created by engineers so that they could communicate with the marketing department and vice versa (Godin, 2001).

Consider some of the implications if this fact is indeed true:

1. Engineers are not teachers, and they are not graphic designers. They are highly logical and scientific thinkers and thus created a supremely rational, linear, non-emotional tool. It follows that this tool, then, may contain built-in structures that are ill-suited for creating compelling stories.
2. The information that was being communicated between these two groups of people was tailored to their particular jobs and needs at that time. PowerPoint was like a visual memo. There was not necessarily a "big idea" accompanied by a call to action. The intent was to be more expository than persuasive. In contrast, staff developers generally present exposition as part of persuasion; they attempt to change the minds of their fellow educators via the presentation and interaction.
3. The program was developed first as an internal, information-sharing mechanism. Who knew it would take the business and education worlds by storm? The built-in backgrounds and templates were not meant to be used by sales representatives, teachers, students, ministers, and others around the globe. Therefore, as staff developers, we are working with a tool not designed with us or our particular audiences in mind.

Getting Started with Software Storyboarding

If you completed the action steps at the end of chapter 2, you should have a hand-sketched/handwritten storyboard of an upcoming presentation with which you can now work at the computer. Remember, as Rick Altman (2007) notes, PowerPoint and other software programs like it are the "wrong tools for the beginning phases of a project, totally wrong. . . . Let's please just acknowledge that these programs are finishing tools, not starting tools" (p. 31).

You should have started with paper, pens, pencils, markers, a white board—whatever you chose to capture your initial thoughts and your first draft. I implore you to follow the same rule I enforced in my tenth-grade English classroom: *do not take up space at a computer unless you have plenty of paper in your hands to work from!* You will create a much better final product if you adhere to this very simple rule.

Reynolds (2008) and Atkinson (2008) offer another guideline that's worth trying to follow: work mostly in slide sorter view (the view where you can see many slides at once, as thumbnails on your screen).

Why is it important for us to try to stay in this view more than in the single-slide, design view? Because when we spend too much time perseverating over individual slides, we can easily lose the big idea. You've probably seen your students (or your own children) take an inordinate amount of time to design one slide, tinkering with the fonts and colors, changing the images, inserting special effects, and so on. That's the "hypnosis" of PowerPoint! It's tempting to sit and craft one slide at a time, incorporating various bells and whistles.

I've started working on a single slide before and then looked up thirty minutes later without much to show for it. I'm sure you have, too. Let's work hard, right now, to prevent that.

Work mostly in slide sorter view. Atkinson (2008) goes far enough to say you should *always* begin working in this view. When you monitor the big picture, your big idea remains the focus.

So, you should have your paper storyboard in hand. Open PowerPoint and create a slate of slides that will be approximately the amount you need, based on the draft you've already completed.

Usually I build a set of twenty to twenty-five slides, all with the default title and bulleted text layout (because design will change later, slide by slide). So my initial, blank, electronic storyboard looks like figure 3.1.

Here are the steps to follow to do the same:

1. Open the PowerPoint program.
2. Create a new, blank presentation (which is the default option).
3. Leave the title slide as it is (it is provided for you). Do not change the background or any other feature.
4. In slide view, on the left side of your screen, click directly under where you now see the title slide. Then above, in the ribbon, click the option "new slide." The program will place a slide with a title placeholder and one

Figure 3.1. Example of Blank PowerPoint Storyboard

bulleted text box under your title slide. Make sure this added slide is highlighted. (You'll see a different color as a border around its edges.)
5. Hit the Ctrl+C keys to copy this new slide.
6. Click under the new slide in slide view and hit Ctrl+V multiple times. Do this until you have pasted nineteen to twenty-four slides into the presentation, still all blank.

Now you have placeholders that you can use to start transferring your rough draft ideas. The next step is choosing a background and appropriate color palette. These decisions are often made quickly and lightly and are to blame for many of the mediocre presentations we see. Don't fall into that trap.

Choosing Your Background and Colors

Design professionals abhor the backgrounds that are graciously provided in PowerPoint, and in most cases, they give ample evidence as to why they feel that way. However, those of us in education probably don't have the time or expertise to create custom backgrounds for our presentations. For that reason, I recommend you either go with a clean, white background (no special features like gradients or fills) or a simple, black background (again, no special features).

Why pure white or black? For starters, they are easy to select. If you open a blank presentation, the default option is plain white. I've found through trial and error that a white background is best for small venues, like a classroom or conference room in a school or central office. Black is best for dimly lit, large venues, like school auditoriums and hotel ballrooms.

Professional designer Nancy Duarte (2008) supports these choices. She says that a dark background is more formal, works better in large venues, and doesn't influence the ambient lighting, whereas a light background is informal, works better in small venues, and helps to illuminate the room (p. 132).

In classrooms, schools, and school office buildings, white backgrounds work very well with the prevalent fluorescent lighting. It's the equivalent of an electronic dry-erase board, and for that reason, perhaps, the white is very comfortable for me to work from—and seems to work well for my audiences.

For keynote address situations, and even in many small hotel conference rooms, my organization's proprietary dark blue background looks polished and professional, while it also is easy on the eyes of my participants. Before using this background, we used a solid black background, and it, too, worked very well in the dimly lit spaces we often found ourselves presenting in.

Duarte (2008) also reminds us to consider a slide show color palette that works well within our profession. For example, in agriculture, the colors of fields (a grassy green) and the sky (a light blue) work well for backgrounds, images, and text (p. 134). For the automotive industry, the colors of asphalt (dark gray), stainless steel (light gray), and lane division lines (bright yellow) may be appropriate (p. 135).

When I'm speaking with educators, I often use a white background with a medium- to dark-blue text and bright, true red as an accent color. This particular pairing, with a little yellow thrown in, basically represents the three primary colors, a palette often used in education. (Think the red apple for the teacher, various bulletin board borders, motivational posters, and that special laser printer paper with the ABC-123 border. Also, think symbols like the ubiquitous apple, the American flag, the little red schoolhouse, and yellow school buses.)

When I use my company's required background of dark blue, my text is white, and there are two approved accent colors that I use quite often, an orange and a yellow. Again, you see how that palette sticks very closely to the primary colors of blue, yellow, and red—and is also generally pleasing to the eyes of most educators.

If you choose a white background, stick with black or blue (or slight variations of these hues) for your text. Consider using bright red as an accent color. In good lighting, the red will immediately draw people's eyes to it because of the high contrast with the white.

If you choose a black background, stick with white or yellow for the main text and consider light, bright green or aqua blue as an accent color. These particular colors seem to "jump out" from the black and draw the audience's eyes to them.

Whatever you do, *choose your palette and stick to it*. Do not add accents of fuchsia or chartreuse if they are not part of your established palette. Don't throw in a slide or two with a leopard-print background, no matter how much you personally like animal prints. The addition of random and/or shocking colors or patterns will visually jar your audience and impede the rapid processing of the information on any given slide.

Keep your overarching goal in mind: to persuade. Anything, even subtle, that distracts from that goal, is your enemy!

If you're considering using one of the backgrounds provided in PowerPoint, or any of the widely available, free, customized ones online, *choose carefully*. Duarte (2008) cautions us, "Backgrounds are a surface for digital assets . . . on which to place elements. They are not in themselves a work of art . . . background creates a sense of space. That space should be open . . . and simple" (p. 118).

Therefore, avoid backgrounds that contain wide borders, lines, texture, or shapes that would be perceived as cutting through or hiding behind your text. Overall, avoid any ornamentation that adds nothing to your meaning. Remember that simplicity is not "dumbing down." Simplicity aids understanding.

Figure 3.2. Example of Ineffective Slide Template

PowerPoint 2007 is much improved over earlier versions, but in figure 3.2 you'll see one of the provided backgrounds that I would not recommend to anyone. The slide background is a medium gray shade with white streaks. Notice how the white streaks are distracting for two reasons: they do not move in the direction our eyes do as we are reading (top left, across to the right, and then down, like an old typewriter with a carriage return). They would visually compete with any text layered on top of them.

Figure 3.3 is a slide made from that template. A teacher used this in a presentation to her fellow high school teachers. The overall color palette (maize yellow title, white body text) provides little contrast. The white text does not sufficiently contrast with the gradient of the background and therefore gets lost (which impedes understanding). And, of course, there are too many bullets and too much text in general. The non-standard bullet is also a bit distracting. While this slide contains excellent information, its visual elements do not aid anyone's understanding of that information.

An abundance of free, online backgrounds also exists for your perusal, but remember—there's a reason they're free. Many of them violate the rules Reynolds,

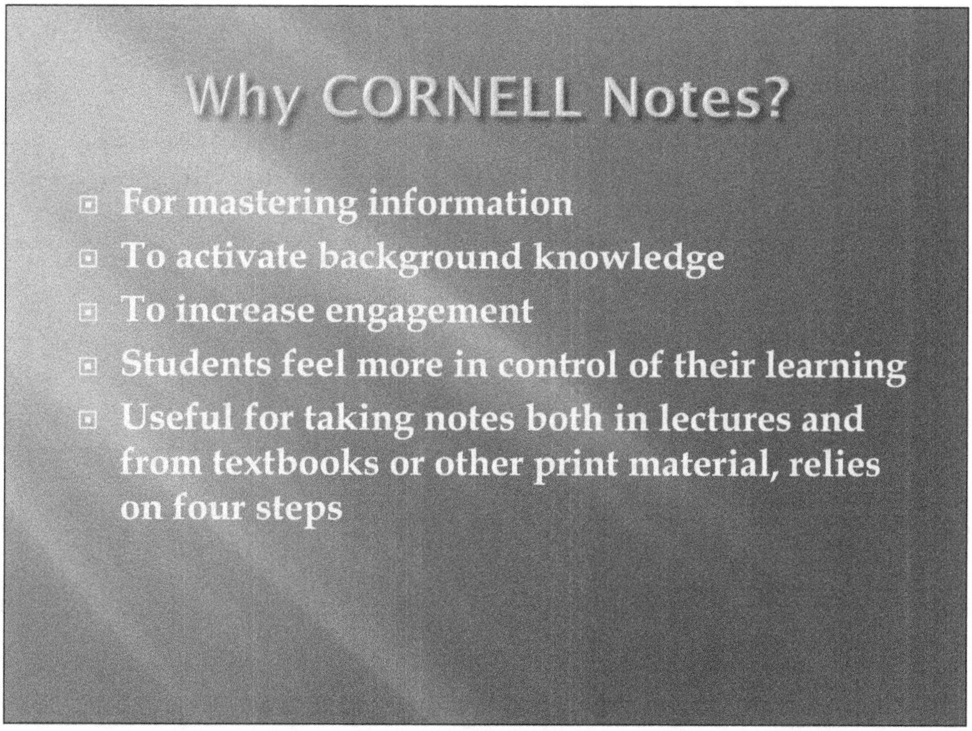

> # Why CORNELL Notes?
>
> - For mastering information
> - To activate background knowledge
> - To increase engagement
> - Students feel more in control of their learning
> - Useful for taking notes both in lectures and from textbooks or other print material, relies on four steps

Figure 3.3. Example of Ineffective Slide Template with Text

Duarte, and others give for visual appeal. For example, how would anyone be able to read your text if you used the background in figure 3.4 (Artist 4, downloaded from http://www.brainybetty.com/PowerPointBackgroundsArtist/artistpowerpointbackgrounds.htm)?

This particular background includes multiple bright colors and looks like shards of broken glass. Both the colors and the shapes could prevent a viewer from quickly digesting any text that would appear on the slide.

Once you've selected a background that doesn't compete with your content and a color palette that will appeal to your audience, it's almost time to start placing content in your slides. Don't rush!

Self-check: *What color palette would be best for your next presentation? Take into consideration the audience and the venue. List some of your ideas.*

Figure 3.4. Example of Ineffective Slide Background

Fonts and Placing Type

Newspapers and magazines no longer actually set type using metal plates, as typesetters did when I first wrote for my high school newspaper. However, some fundamentals of font selection and placement of text remain with us from those days past, and for good reason—they make a page look good! As you're designing a PowerPoint presentation, the same principles apply to any individual slide, and a major part of the visual appeal is dependent upon the color, size, and styles of typefaces (fonts) that you use.

In PowerPoint 2007, the new default font is Calibri, which comes in two weights, one for headings, and one for body text. Calibri is a perfectly fine font, but if you want to differentiate your presentations from millions of others, you'll want to consider selecting a different body font, and perhaps in addition, a secondary font to use for headings.

Occasionally, you may want to use a third font for impact, as I did when I made the slide in figure 3.5 to emphasize a key point in a presentation I was making about (what else?) giving good presentations! I used Calibri for the attribution, but Impact (in point size 72) for the quotation itself. Impact does make quite a statement because of its bold strokes and thick weight.

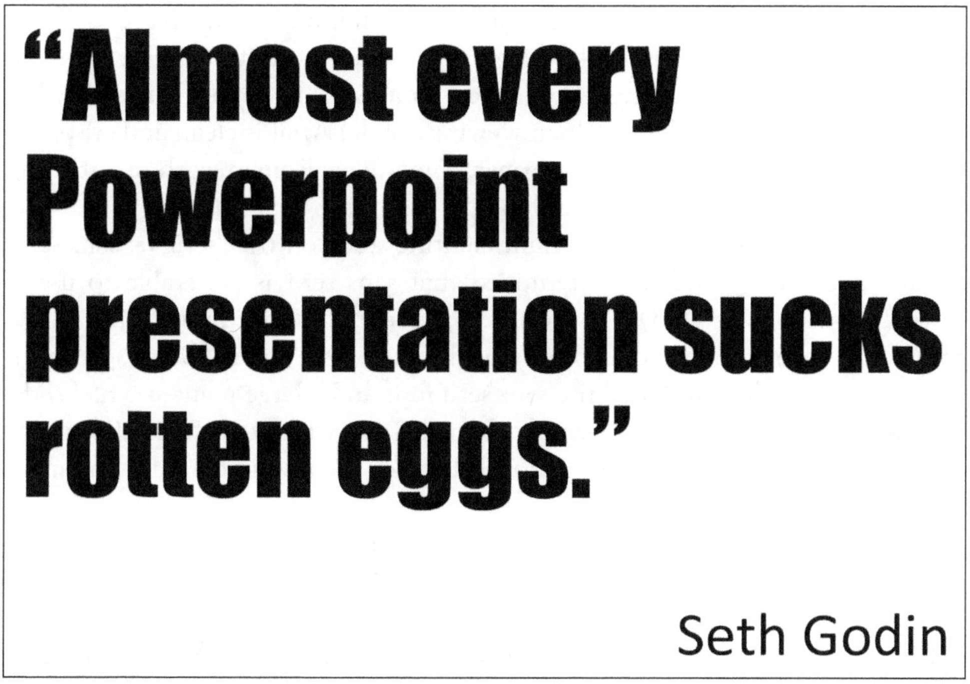

> **"Almost every Powerpoint presentation sucks rotten eggs."**
>
> Seth Godin

Figure 3.5. Example of Using Large Text for Impact

So, what do you need to know about fonts? My husband actually calls me "the font police" because of my passionate disdain for poorly designed brochures, signs, invitations, and handouts. However, you probably don't need (or want) to know as much about fonts as I do in order to make beautiful and effective PowerPoint slides.

Here's some quick advice from the font police. The main thing you need to know is about serifs. Serifs are the tips on the ends of letters, or more thoroughly, "any of the short lines stemming from and at an angle to the upper and lower ends of the strokes of a letter" (Merriam Webster Online Dictionary, 2009). Fonts like Times New Roman and Courier New, both available in PowerPoint and Word, have these little tips. In contrast, fonts like Arial and Verdana, two personal favorites, are "sans serif" fonts and do not have these little tips.

Basically, serif fonts are often used when there is a large amount of text to process, because the little tips help our eyes stay focused on the same line and sweep more text into our visual field at a time. They are ideal for your handouts, but not usually for your slides for this very reason.

Sans serif fonts have letters that are usually fatter with more open space, like Impact, mentioned and shown above. San serif fonts are better for small amounts of text and are often used for billboards, newspaper headlines, and in children's books.

If you abide by the "less is more" guideline pertaining to the presence of text on a slide, then you will probably want to choose a sans serif font. The company I work for uses Arial bold, size 24 or higher, for all slide text, and Times New Roman, size 12, for all handouts. When viewing a slide, Arial is clean and crisp, and it gets the point across quickly. On paper, Times New Roman, with its little serif "feet," keeps our eyes rolling right along.

Duarte (2008) recounts her own unscientific study on the "serif vs. sans serif" debate in *Slideology* and has determined that sans serif is preferable to use in PowerPoint shows (p. 143). I'm with her! I recently attended a national educators' conference and went to two sessions that had more than 2000 people in the room. The presenter that used the sans serif font and a large point size had slides that were far more visually appealing than the one who used the serif font and roughly the same point size, even though both of them were cursed with far too much text on each slide.

Study this slide in figure 3.6 from a presentation that I made about Garr Reynolds' work. When displayed in color, it is mostly light blue with a green leaf, and the text is in black. You'll notice the entire slide is filled with an image. The text is Calibri in bold, size 42. What if I had chosen a serif font instead? For example,

Figure 3.6. Effective Font and Image Combination

Figure 3.7. Ineffective Font and Image Combination

see Times New Roman in point size 40 in figure 3.7. How is the overall aesthetic different?

There's a reason Calibri is the default font in PowerPoint. It looks good when large and projected. And there's a reason most books and magazines you read are in Times New Roman or something similar: because the text looks good small and in long lines. The artistry of fonts enhances your eye's abilities to take the message in as rapidly as possible.

The best resource I recommend as a "mini-course" on fonts in general is Robin Williams' *The Non-Designer's Design Book*, third edition (2008). This book is an excellent guide on the nuances of different fonts and will help you create visually pleasing handouts, brochures, flyers, and other documents that, as an educator, you may often have the opportunity to create. Additionally, the author has a very conversational tone and a lovely dry wit. Her books are a joy to read.

One last note—or rather, a plea—about fonts. *Teachers, stop using Comic Sans!* It's just not cute anymore. Use it with your students, if you like (but please make it point size 14 or larger, for better reading). Please don't use it for the parent newsletter, a memo, an e-mail, or God forbid, a handout at a state, regional, or national conference. Comic Sans is fine in small doses, but it looks juvenile and unprofessional when you have it as your "signature" font. Find another, more grown-up sans serif font, like Arial, Tahoma, or Verdana.

> *Self-check: Select one or two fonts for the presentation you're about to design. Why did you choose these particular fonts? How do they coordinate with your color palette and your content; in other words, why are they a "best fit"?*

Other Effects

As you watch television news or sports, how do your eyes react when a graphic or words come flying onto the screen? Generally, our eyes go toward the movement. It's the same with a PowerPoint show.

As Rick Altman (2007) notes, "When something moves on screen, your audience has no choice but to watch it" (p. 20). Therefore, if you use an animation or a slide transition, do it with purpose. Because your audience's eyes are forced to pay attention to movement, use it *only if it enhances your point*.

Nancy Duarte (2008) says it this way: "It's tempting to make everything buzz like a fly or swoosh like a rocket. Don't do it" (p. 180). Stephen Kosslyn, in *Clear and to the Point* (2007), goes even further, saying, "Every visible or auditory change should convey information" (p. 10).

As educators, we have often been concerned about capturing and maintaining our students' attention, and because of that concern, we may have developed some bad habits, like having our text enter with the typing sound effect, or using different transitions throughout a presentation so that students will wonder, "What will happen next? The checkerboard or a wipe left? Hmmm."

It's not that we did these things with bad intentions, but we need to be more strategic as we design our presentations for our adult audiences. We simply must stick to our core message and design each image, each movement, and each sound to support it, not to detract from it.

If you do use bullet points (and surely, on some slides, you will), consider having the bullets appear "on click." This is a command in PowerPoint, and it's quite appropriate to use as you direct your participants' attention to your points, one by one.

Again, Duarte offers some pertinent advice: "Hide elements until you need to refer to them. This ensures [that] the item being discussed will remain the focus . . . resulting in the audience listening more and reading less" (p. 183).

While some other experts disagree with Duarte, I have employed the "bullet on-click" guideline quite successfully over the past two years and find that people are far less busy trying to copy all the words on the slide when I do so. They are more focused on participating in the discussion when I guide their attention in this very explicit way.

As for slide transitions, you have the option in PowerPoint to set "no transition" as your default, and I suggest you do this. If you must use transitions at any point in your presentation, using a simple fade or wipe is usually best. Please don't use random transitions for the same reason you don't use random effects. You don't want the audience members' brains to be asking, "What will happen next?" You want their brains to be getting ever closer to the "a-ha" or the realization of the big idea.

Another useful caveat comes from Altman (2007): avoid the "recency of discovery" (p. 13). This is when you have just learned to do something in PowerPoint, like adding an animation effect, and you use it, perhaps repeatedly, regardless of whether or not it fits the message or the task. My high school students were masters of recency of discovery, loading their presentations with the cash register sound, zooming clip art, bouncing graphics, and so on.

Don't allow yourself to be misled into using recency of discovery, or you run the risk of your audience remembering all of the wrong things and none of the right things.

Start Transferring Your Storyboard

It's time now, with your sketches and notes in hand, to place information on your blank slides. First, take the bird's-eye view you have in slide sorter, and mark off sections. For example, if I have a presentation that includes three key points, I go in at first and create separator slides, also sometimes called bumper slides, to denote each section break. I simply write a note to myself on those slides, and make the point size large enough that I can see it well in slide sorter view at all times. So a bumper slide might look something like figure 3.8.

Atkinson's (2008) method of drafting begins with building three sections and color-coding them in slide sorter view before you begin putting any content or graphics on your slides (p. 69). If this method appeals to you, by all means, do it. Just remember to undo the color-coding by selecting one background (that doesn't compete with your content, graphics, or big idea) when you are finished so your final product has a unified, professional feel—not a hodgepodge of colors. I don't do the color-coding myself because it's one less thing for me to clean up later.

> # Section on writing process starts here

Figure 3.8. Example of a Bumper Slide

At this point in the creation, don't obsess over the sizes or colors of the text or about choosing the perfect image for any slide. *Just transfer your ideas to the slides.* You will go back and refine the individual slides later.

A note about text: consider keeping all body text at point size 30 or higher in this first pass. At this size, you will be limited in how much text you place on a slide, and you'll be assured that the text is easily readable from anywhere in the room in almost every venue.

If you have any given slide on which you are trying to place text that is size 24 or smaller, you may be trying to create a slide out of material that should really be in your handout instead. Ask yourself, what's the key point here? How can I represent it in as few words as possible? Or you might ask yourself, can I represent the key point with no words at all and with a compelling image instead? Rick Altman (2007) would say that if you can do that, you've found "the holy grail of presenting" (p. 17).

If you use any clip art at all (and most experts recommend that you don't), consider small images or symbols that recur to denote sections in your presentation, or to indicate an activity that will recur. For example, the image of the key in figure 3.9 appears with each key point in one of the presentations I sometimes give. The key would be even better if it were a photographic image instead of clip art. This presentation is one that many presenters in my organization give, however, and at the time it was created, we did not have access to a photographic image that we could use.

You may or may not have access or the funding to use a large number of strong photographs. If that's the case, the judicious use of high-quality clip art is permissible.

If you know you want a visual image on any slide (you should have roughed these out on your hand-done storyboard), then put a placeholder there, or a note to yourself. Just don't waste time obsessing over finding the perfect image quite yet.

Figure 3.9. Use of a Recurring Symbol to Denote Content

The same advice applies to representing data. If you have spaces where you intend to use a graph or chart, don't start designing that visual quite yet. Just put one of the Smart Art graphics on your slide as a placeholder, and jot a note to yourself. You will come back to this later.

In short, as simply and quickly as possible, transfer what you see on your paper to what you're looking at on the screen.

With text, avoid complete sentences if you are using slides with bullets. Aim for "headlines" or phrases. Strive to be parallel in your bullets (but you can fix that later too). With images, put in placeholders or substitute images if you can't quickly find what you need in the final product. During the revision and editing phase, you can improve the visual appeal of text, empty space, images, and data.

> *Self-check: How many slides have you created? What percentage of these slides rely mostly on text to express your ideas? Can you reduce the percentage? If so, how? On slides with bulleted text, can you reduce the words and/or the number of bullets? If so, how?*

48　～　Chapter Three

Let the Data Speak!

Surely at some point, you will need to represent data on at least one slide. Just as you want any slide with text or a visual image on it to speak volumes about the subject matter instantly, so do you want your graphs, charts, and tables to do the same.

Remember that data slides are not really about the data. They are about the *meaning* you are trying to convey, or the story of the data (Duarte, 2008, p. 64). Your data must be displayed clearly and must be in direct support of your core message. Duarte (2008) reminds us to "keep it simple" when displaying data (p. 65). That means the simpler the display, the larger the chart or graph, and the clearer the main point of the data, the better that slide is.

Pie charts and bar charts are two graphics that work very well with most data. Line graphs or scatter plots are also sometimes desirable. *Avoid three-dimensional data displays.* These do nothing to simplify the data or support your point more clearly; they add only extraneous visual detail.

In figures 3.10 through 3.12, look at the pie chart makeover and options.

See in the original how the patterns of the pie slices compete with each other for attention? Which pie slices are we supposed to be looking at? They are all

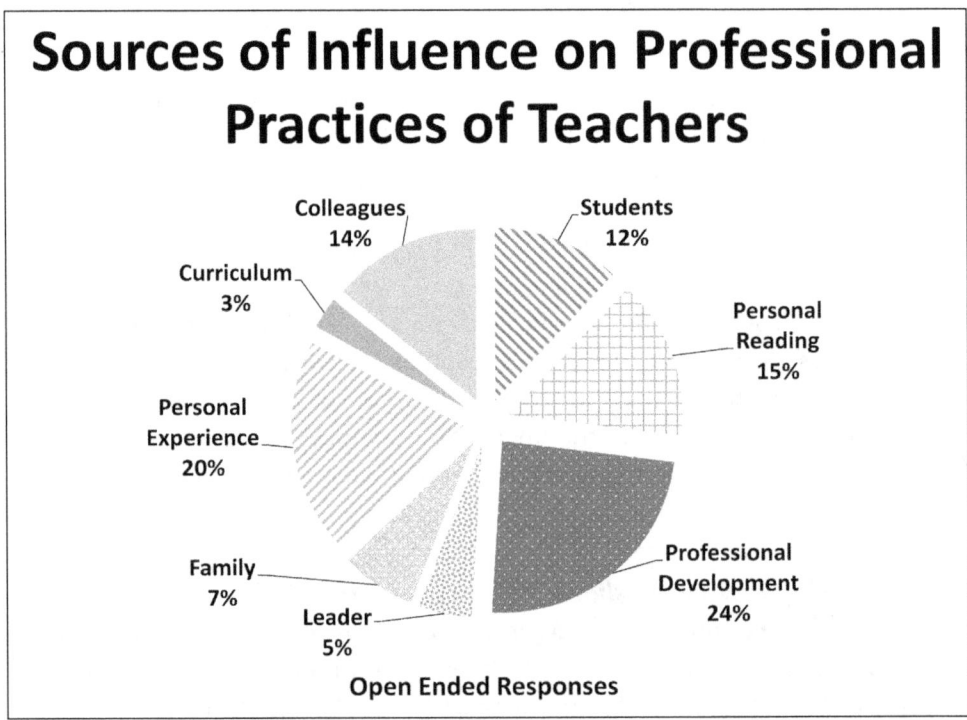

Figure 3.10.　Ineffective Pie Chart

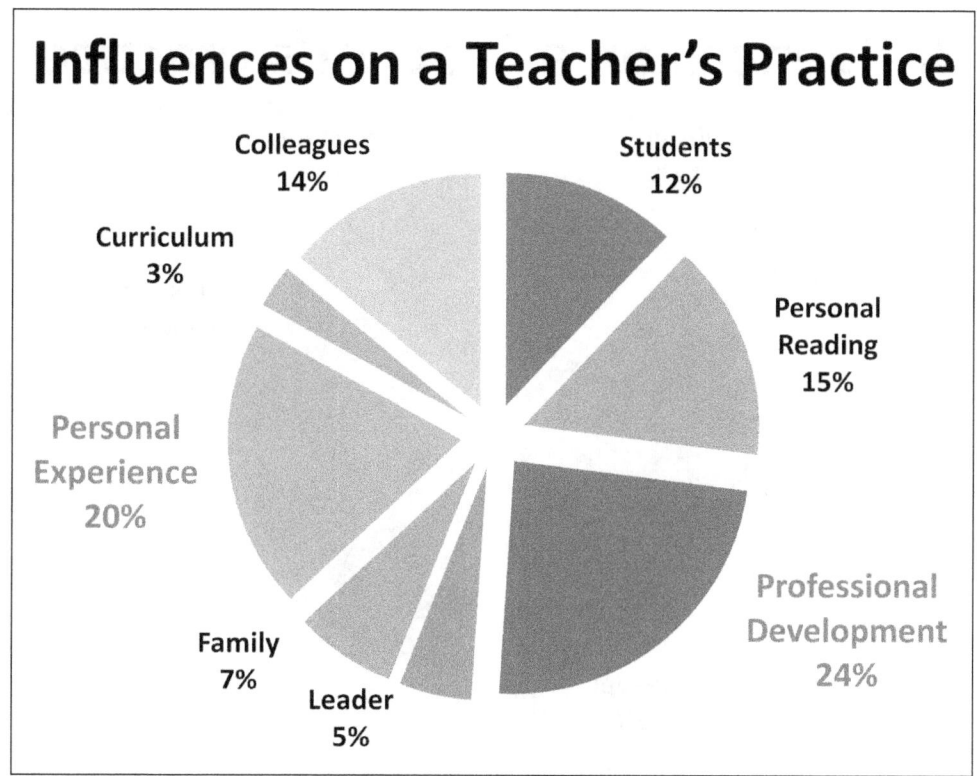

Figure 3.11.   Effective Pie Chart

different colors and patterns. It's not clear what the speaker's message is with this slide, and the amount of text also interferes with the point we are supposed to grasp.

Now let's perform a simple makeover of the slide, reducing the text, making the overall graphic larger, and using solid-color pie slices instead. I also colored the text of ideas that I want to call attention to in light blue and made the font size larger for those particular pieces (Personal Experience, Professional Development).

If I had chosen to use a three-dimensional pie chart instead, the slide would appear as figure 3.12. This particular effect makes the slices appear further apart, but it does not add to the visual impact of the data. The simplest, largest pie chart is the best of the three possible options here.

Enhancing Your Message with Photographic Images

Remember that you are telling a story with your presentation. How did you first learn come to understand stories as a child—through the spoken word, through

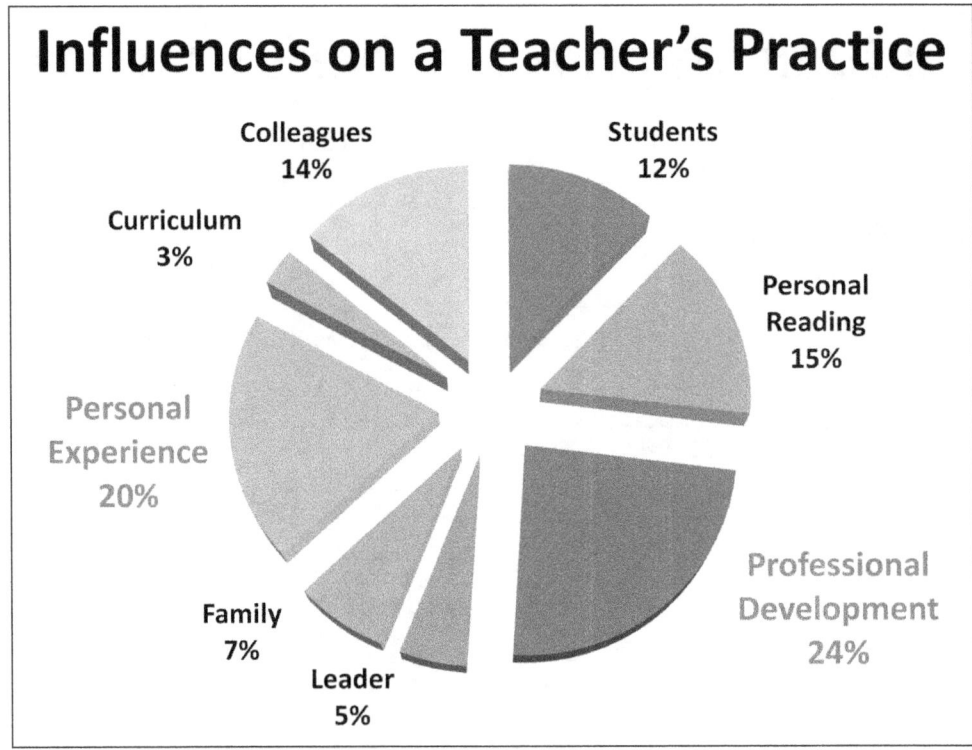

Figure 3.12. Use of 3-D with Pie Chart

the printed word, or through sights, sounds, and pictures? Dan Pink (2006) reminds us in *A Whole New Mind* that facts are widely available and very easily accessible; it is now more important to place them in context and to deliver them with emotional impact than it was in the past (p. 103).

To give your presentations emotional punch, consider following my "rules" for images, outlined below, as you continue to tinker with the electronic draft you are creating.

Angela's Rules for Images
1. *More images, fewer words*. This can mean creating far more slides than you are accustomed to! There is no "right" or "wrong" number of slides.

    Nancy Duarte says the viewer should be able to process a slide in three seconds. That's a good rule of thumb for processing the slide but not necessarily for how long to display it. You can display any given slide for as long as you need to do the teaching that goes with that slide. Just be aware that for even a short professional learning session of an hour, you could have fifty or more slides if your images are used well and your teaching-learning activities are planned well.

Look at the examples in figures 3.13 and 3.14. Which slide is more appealing? Which slide forces you to listen to the speaker and to participate in the conversation?

2. *Give credit where credit's due. Don't steal images.* Use Morguefile.com for free images and IStockPhoto.com for purchased images.

You cannot simply Google a topic and use the images you find without permission from the copyright holder. If so, you are a plagiarist.

Also you may want to check out http://www.freeimages.co.uk. Be aware of what constitutes plagiarism with images just as you would expect your students to.

3. *Avoid clip art.* Yes, we teachers love Christmas sweaters, bulletin board trim, special printer paper with borders of apples or pencils, and lots of other items with cute, cartoonish images—but there are very few acceptable reasons to put these cheesy images in presentations you will be giving to other adults.

Other than using a simple image as an icon to break up sections or to alert your audience (visually) to special information, there are very few reasons to employ clip art.

Use your powerful teaching to make an impact and forget about clip art that doesn't help you advance your ideas.

4. *Don't distort photo images.* Use *only* the diagonal pull handles if you resize a photo. Be aware when resizing of the quality (pixels) of your image; it can get fuzzy. You need sharp images.

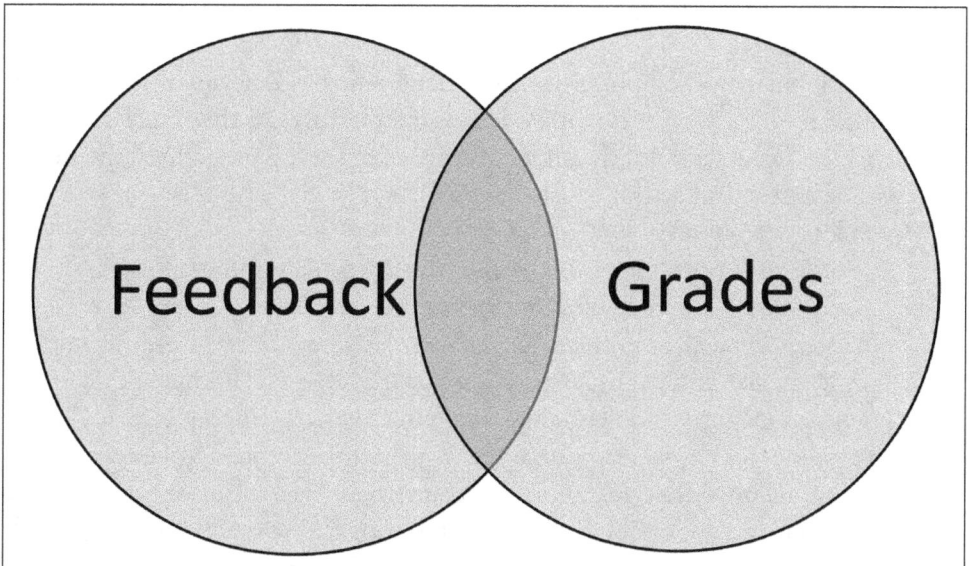

Figure 3.13. Venn Diagram instead of Bulleted Text

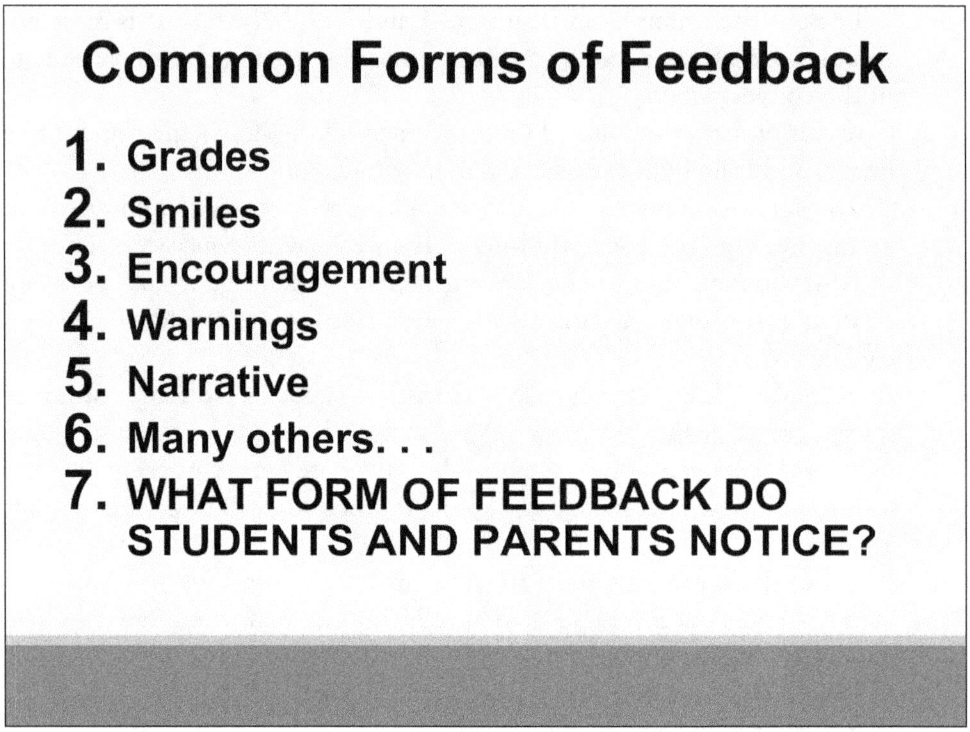

Common Forms of Feedback

1. **Grades**
2. **Smiles**
3. **Encouragement**
4. **Warnings**
5. **Narrative**
6. **Many others...**
7. **WHAT FORM OF FEEDBACK DO STUDENTS AND PARENTS NOTICE?**

Figure 3.14. Numbered Text instead of Venn Diagram

Crop unnecessary parts of the image before placing on the slide if you need to. Use the cropping to make your photo subjects as large and as striking as possible.

In many cases, emphasizing faces heightens the emotional appeal. Rick Altman (2007) gives this tip: When using photos, size them to 1024 pixels wide to fit the width of the slide. Make sure to set the program so the height will adjust automatically with this width (p. 208). This easy tip will save you lots of trouble.

Strive to avoid a common offense, the distorted photograph with people who look they are in the fun mirrors at the carnival.

5. *No useless animation, entrances, exits, or transitions.* Human eyes pay attention to movement, as discussed earlier in this chapter. Enough said!
6. *Use video sparingly.* You can use video effectively to emphasize a key point, to provide humor, to lead into a break, or to bring a break to an end. However, remember that the more technical bells and whistles you add, the more that can go wrong as you are presenting. So you will have to provide the information that the video would have if for some reason the clip does not work during your presentation.

Also, you must be very aware of volume and lighting when using video clips. Ensure that everyone can see and hear what you are showing by previewing the clips during your presentation setup phase.

And, as with photographs, avoid violating copyright laws by using clips that are restricted.

7. *White (empty) space is a valuable commodity.* It needs to be used with intention. It should not be an afterthought.

Nancy Duarte (2008) urges us to consider taking away anything that won't change the meaning and to consider splitting heavy content across several slides (p. 106).

There's a reason magazines and books have margins. There's a reason cities have parks. People's eyes and spirits need "resting space." Give it to them.

Time to Revise and Edit

The directions on shampoo bottles often say to lather, rinse, and repeat. Duarte's (2008) advice for this stage in the development of your presentation is similar: reduce, record, and repeat (p. 221).

First, start practicing the presentation with the slides you have now created. (Duarte recommends that you record yourself by audio or video as you do this.) Go through the entire deck without stopping to revise, narrating as if you are giving the presentation live.

Jot quick notes, by hand or in the speaker's notes section under each slide, in any places where you feel you either lack information or where you feel that you spend too much time or provide too much detail. These are areas where you can revise after the first run-through.

After the first run-through, sit down with your draft. Reduce the amount of text on slides so that you are left with only keywords or phrases that trigger your narration. Break large chunks of information into smaller chunks across several slides. Insert these blank slides and note what kind of visual image or keywords you may want to use in the final version of them.

Go ahead after this first out-loud delivery and insert some of your visual images and representations of data. Get your draft in good working order for your second, out-loud delivery. If you did record your first delivery, study this attempt before you make your second.

Now it's time to record again. *Do your second real delivery.* Your slides should now be in a form that lends itself to a delivery pretty close to what the real thing will be. Do as smooth and complete of a run-through as possible.

If necessary, jot quick notes about changes you want to make to the slides. Then take time later to make your changes.

After this second, solid run-through, you should have a visual presentation that needs only minor tweaks. You should also have a recorded version of the presentation that you can continue to review right up until the day you present to your intended audience.

Never forget to run spell-check and grammar-check before you display your PowerPoint for others. I generally also ask either my husband or a colleague (whoever is handier and more likely to say yes) to look over my slides before I present them.

You will never forgive yourself if you have a misspelled word or the wrong word displayed on a screen, ten feet high, and an audience member points it out to you—or, worse yet, you realize the error but become flustered when you see it. You don't want to lose your cool or compromise your credibility—so extra proofreading is always in your best interest! Your audience will also appreciate the fact that you took the time and care to create a flawless presentation.

A Short Workshop in Slide Design

Garr Reynolds (2005) says, "Never decorate your messages or your supporting visuals. Decoration is veneer. Think design, but never decoration. Design is soul deep, decoration is 'Happy Birthday' placed atop a sponge cake" (http://presentationzen.blogs.com/presentationzen/2005/10/make_your_next_.html). Using what you have learned about basic design in this chapter, complete the following exercises.

Figure 3.15 is a visual image (a photograph) with text placed on top of it. This kind of layering technique is easy to do in PowerPoint. It forces the audience to pay close attention to the speaker for the accompanying information. Examine your slides. Is there a place where you could do something similar?

Figure 3.16 is a powerful quote that serves as a key point in a seminar on creating common formative assessments. What ideas do you have for representing this idea in a more visually appealing way?

Figure 3.17 is one remake of the slide. Notice the emotion in the graduate's face, the larger point size of the text, and the complete citation now on the slide. Doesn't this slide make the point in a much more emotionally engaging way?

Figure 3.18 is a slide from a workshop that I teach frequently. Notice that the purpose of the slide is to define a concept called Data Teams. Data Teams are a form of collaboration advocated by the organization I work for, The Leadership and Learning Center. How could this slide rely less on text and more on a visual, while still imparting the necessary information? Can you sketch out a more visually appealing idea?

One idea for revising the slide appears in figure 3.19. This is a photographic image, cropped a bit from the bottom, with text layered on top. This particular

Figure 3.15. Example of Text Placed on Image

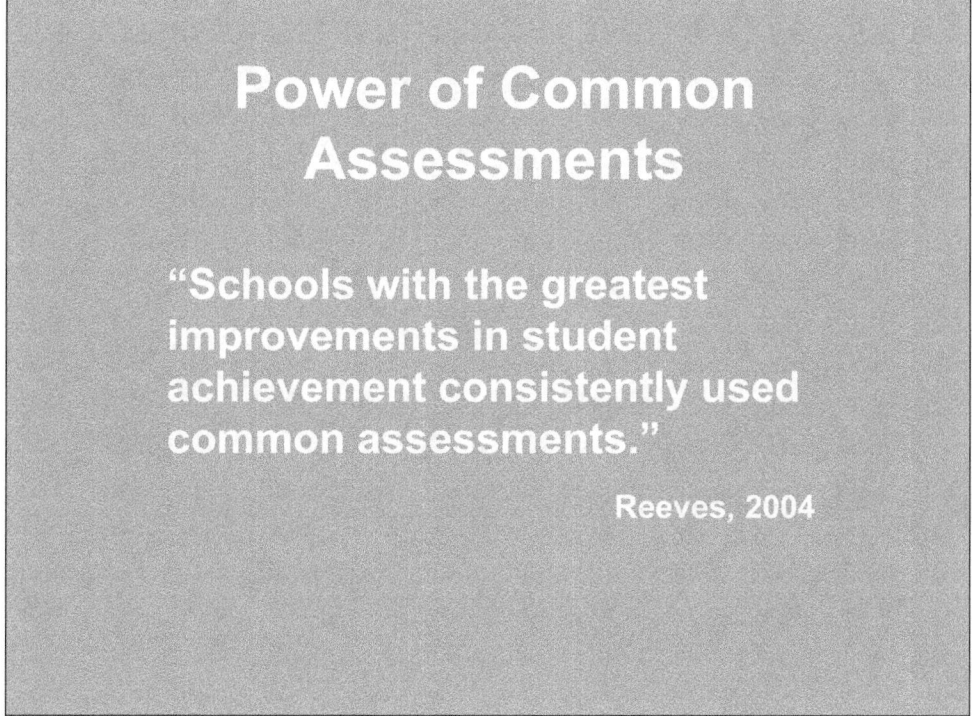

Figure 3.16. Important Point in Text

> "Schools with the greatest improvements in student achievement consistently used common assessments."
>
> D. Reeves, *Accountability in Action*, 2004

Figure 3.17. Important Point with Text and Image

What Are Data Teams?

- Small grade-level or department teams that examine individual student work generated from common formative assessments
- Collaborative, structured, scheduled meetings that focus on the effectiveness of teaching and learning

Figure 3.18. Definition in Text

A Picture Is Worth a Thousand Words ~ 57

Figure 3.19. Definition with Text and Image

photographic image is well suited for text on the bottom because the surface of the table is plain and has a texture that works well with text and doesn't compete with it.

See the slide in figure 3.20. One of the chief problems is the distortion of the images. Notice how the two photos to the right, in particular, don't look natural. How might you revise this slide? Other than adjusting the photos, what other improvements could be made?

Which of the following two slides in figures 3.21 and 3.22 would you prefer to use in your presentation? Why? Can you name the design elements that make one preferable to the other?

Sometimes the content of a slide could be better represented on a handout. See the following two examples in figures 3.23 and 3.24. These slides give direction for an activity that occurred in a workshop but did not need to be projected if the audience had a handout. They are more appropriate to appear only in the handout and not on the screen.

Consider this visual image in figure 3.25, which is a Microsoft stock image and free for all users of PowerPoint. What could it symbolize? In how many ways could it be used?

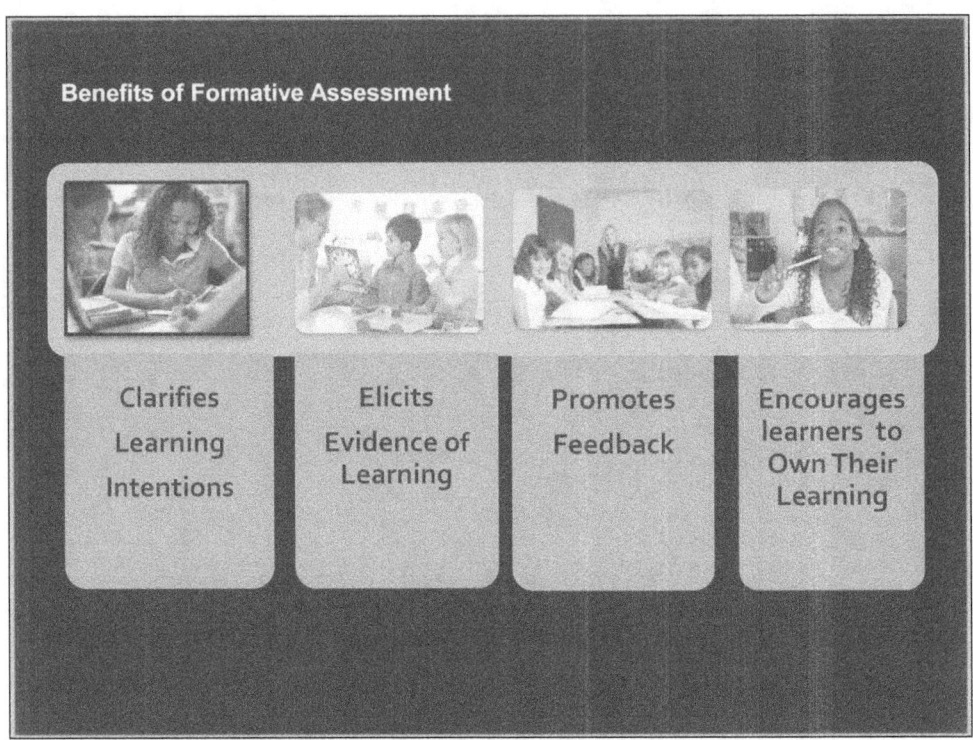

Figure 3.20. Example of Distorted Image

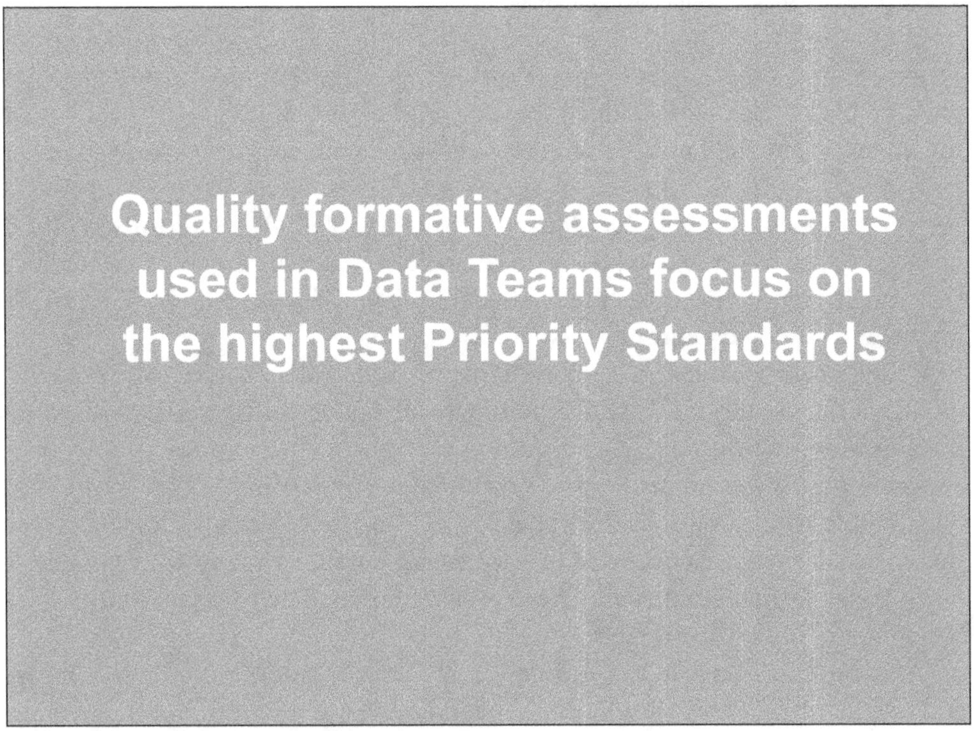

Quality formative assessments used in Data Teams focus on the highest Priority Standards

Figure 3.21. Information in Text

Data Teams focus only on priority standards.

Figure 3.22. Information with Text and Image

1-Minute Reflection
COOPERATIVE LEARNING

Think about a time when, either as a student or a teacher, you engaged in a cooperative learning activity that increased your learning significantly.

Figure 3.23. Example of Giving Directions 1

3-Minute Pair Share
COOPERATIVE LEARNING

- Discuss what you recalled during your one-minute reflection with a partner close by.
- What characteristics do your stories share?

Figure 3.24. Example of Giving Directions 2

Figure 3.25. Powerful Image 1

Figure 3.26. Powerful Image 2. *Source:* Morguefile.com.

Figure 3.27. Powerful Image 3. *Source:* Morguefile.com.

I've used that particular image to represent collaboration. Another image I could use is figure 3.26, of geese flying in formation. I could add anecdotal information here about how the flapping of each bird's wings creates lift which helps to carry the entire flock. A powerful visual along with a supportive story can create a stronger impact with the audience.

If I wanted to demonstrate more of a classroom or student-oriented form of collaboration, I could use an image like figure 3.27.

Action Steps

1. With your handwritten/drawn storyboard in hand, storyboard next in PowerPoint, using the slide sorter view as much as possible. Follow the guidelines presented in this chapter. Leave placeholders on slides where you will insert photographic images. You will search for images that mirror your hand-done draft in step 2.
2. Create a folder of images that go with the big idea and key points of your presentation. Search Microsoft Online first, as these have no restrictions. Then check out free sites like Morguefile.com and search.

    Don't limit yourself to images only directly related to education; for example, nature imagery, sports and recreation imagery, and other categories can represent your topics well. And don't forget to represent your points by using metaphors and analogies.

    If you have done your storyboarding by hand in a creative, free-flowing manner, you will not be restricted in searching for images, because your mind will have explored several ways to do this. Think from the novice's mind.
3. Place images in the slides. Leave placeholders where you need to represent data. You will go back and do your charts and graphs later.
4. Set your background, text, and colors. Do NOT use the backgrounds provided in the program, unless you use pure black or pure white.

    Use a sans serif font with titles (if you must use them on slides) as large as possible. I prefer size 54 for titles, and Arial or Calibri. Other good choices: Tahoma, Verdana.

    Stop using Comic Sans. It looks childish. Use it with your students if you must, but not with other adults.

    Some good backgrounds are out there for free—but be careful. See the following sites, but be choosy:

    http://www.brainybetty.com/NewPowerPointBackgroundswithSidebars/index.htm

    http://www.brainybetty.com/DoubleFades2004/index.htm

http://www.brainybetty.com/LiveMeetingTemplates256/index.htm
http://brainybetty.com/NotebookBacks2006/Notebook_Backgrounds.htm

This one is for students but has a clean, crisp look:

http://office.microsoft.com/en-us/templates/TC101671251033.aspx?CategoryID=CT101450441033.

Self-check: Although they are not by any means of low quality, the following slides in figures 3.28 through 3.31 could be improved. Examine each one and record your ideas for revisions. Base your revisions on guidelines given in this chapter.

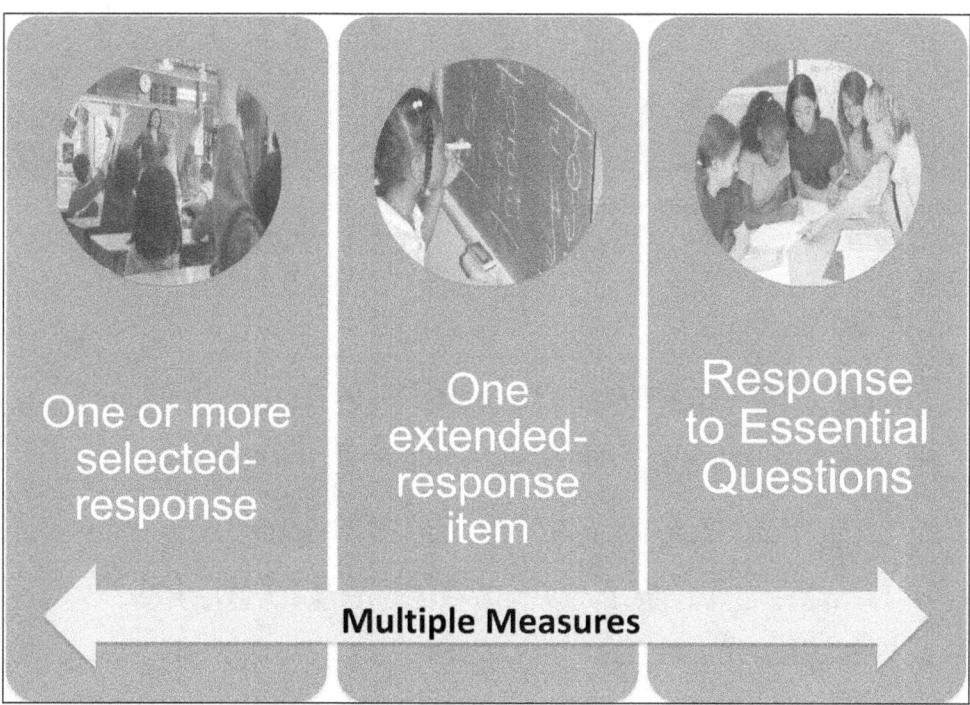

Figure 3.28. Slide That Needs Improvement 1

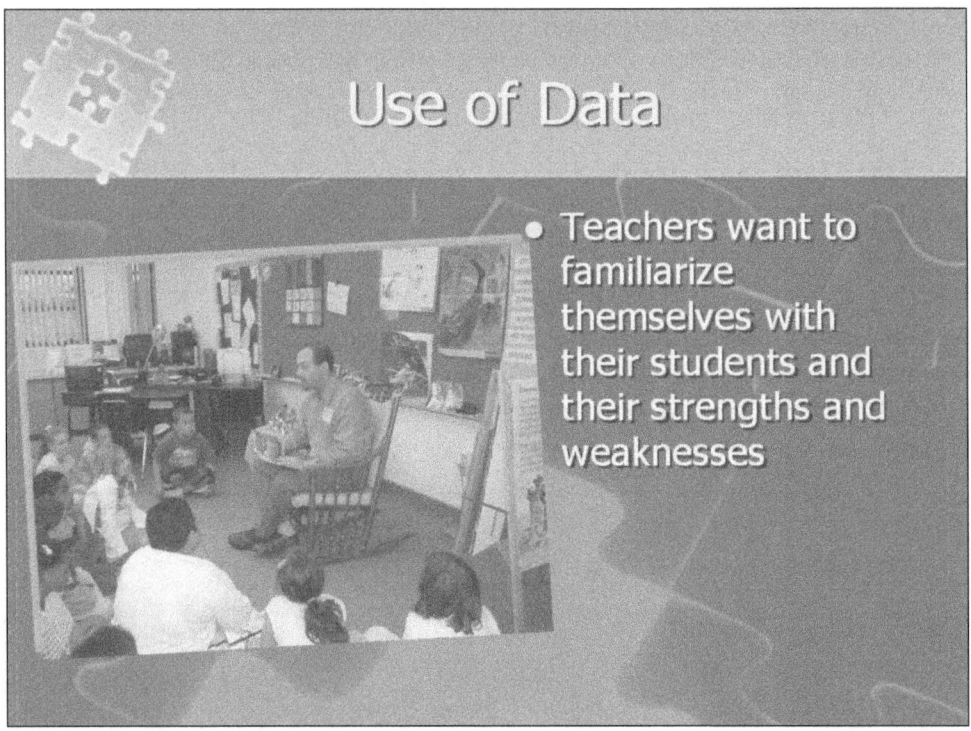

Figure 3.29. Slide That Needs Improvement 2

I want to develop readers who...

- *Find a place for reading in their lives.*
- *Enjoy reading and its challenges.*
- *Utilize a variety of strategies to make sense of texts.*
- *Are willing and able to generate, articulate, and negotiate interpretations.*
- *Become emotionally invested in what they read.*

Figure 3.30. Slide That Needs Improvement 3

5 Rules of Thumb for Maintaining Balance
Dr. Dorothy Strickland, IRA & NUA

1. Teach skills as a way to gain **meaning**. Skills are not ends in themselves.

2. Each day, include time for both **guided instruction & independent work**. Otherwise, students will never internalize skills and make them their own.

3. Avoid teaching children as if they were empty receptacles for knowledge. Instead, allow them to build knowledge in a **process-oriented** way.

4. Integrate print and electronic materials effectively. That way, your classroom will reflect the **multimedia** world in which students live.

5. Always consider standardized test scores in light of *__informal assessment data__ (*Note: *individual assessment data*).

Figure 3.31.   Slide That Needs Improvement 4

CHAPTER FOUR

Be Prepared

"Be prepared" is the motto of the Boy Scouts, but it applies to the work of staff developers, too. Just as in classroom teaching, you never know what might happen during a presentation you are giving. Thus, you must be prepared physically and mentally for any contingency.

In this chapter, you'll find suggestions for being ready to address anything that might happen—before, during, and after your presentation. At the end of the chapter, you'll find several real scenarios for reflection. Also, as in other chapters, you'll find action steps to implement.

What Does It Truly Mean to Be Prepared?

The Boy Scout motto "be prepared" applies to both spirit and body. Being prepared as a speaker is no different. Your head has to be in the game fully, and your body needs to be, too. Take some steps to prepare them both beforehand, and you'll be a much better speaker than you have been in the past.

To be prepared in mind, you must know your material inside and out. You must have real examples and anecdotes to offer to make the story come alive. You must anticipate the questions and confusions your audience may have. It is your job to preempt those as fully as you can, and to address them directly and knowledgeably when they do arise.

At all times, you must be the epitome of grace, level-headedness, and professionalism. Therefore, the more often you envision the presentation itself, including the possible reactions of your participants, the more inwardly prepared you will be when you actually start talking.

You must also be able to present your information in a compelling manner even if all technology is absent. Ideally, you should be able to teach with nothing more than chalk and a board, or markers and paper, or your voice and the active listening of your attendees.

To be prepared physically involves both you as a person and also your environmental surroundings. You must have energy and enthusiasm and plan to be seen and heard throughout the session.

Nothing in your attire or manner should distract from your core message being internalized. The setting must be as comfortable and as conducive to learning as possible. You must plan both mentally and physically for interaction among the participants; if the room is too small to allow for small group discussions and movement, it is not acceptable. You will have to find innovative solutions to problems like that (and to many problems you would least expect).

Just as a classroom teacher knows the fire evacuation route, the steps to take during a tornado alert, where the closest bathrooms are, and when lunch is served, so will you have to know the details that impact the physical, social, and learning needs of your participants. The lighting, heat, air conditioning, background noise, size of the screen, comfort of the chairs, arrangement of the tables, and other environmental concerns must be controlled as much as possible.

> ***Self-check:** When you have been a participant in professional development sessions, what exactly about the presenter as a person has supported your learning? What exactly about the learning environment has supported your learning? What can you learn from these examples?*

To be fully prepared seems like a tall order, doesn't it? In the sections that follow, I'll provide specific suggestions that I've shared as I've taught other staff developers to improve their craft. Nothing is fictional here and is shared in hopes that you can be proactive.

If You're Just Starting to Make Presentations

If you're just starting out in your professional developer's role, allow me to make some suggestions for your own long-term success.

First, there are some purchases you can make that will serve you well if you plan to have this role for a year or more. Two items that you need immediately are a remote slide advancer (a "clicker") and a device that helps you call any large group back to order (for example, a bell, chime, or whistle). The remotes usually plug into a USB port on your computer and can be operated from as far as fifty feet away; this allows you to circulate and present from any part of the room without having to walk back to your computer keyboard to go to the next slide in your PowerPoint. Of course, with a bell, chime, whistle, or other device used to gain the attention of your audience, you will need to be in close proximity to folks so they can hear the cue.

Take some time to decide on exactly what style of each of these items that you might prefer. If possible, experiment with a colleague's clicker before you purchase one, and observe the tools that other speakers use when restoring quietness in a session. (Many people use the raised hand signal or a countdown from five to one, but these two methods just don't work for me. Try them and see if they work for you, as they require no equipment—just your hands and voice!)

Ideally, a clicker should be as small as possible so that your audience can hardly tell you have it in your hand. This was a big challenge for me, as my hands are very small. The first two remotes that I purchased, even though fairly small, didn't allow me to easily hold them and flip through note cards simultaneously. They both worked fine to advance slides, but they just didn't make me feel comfortable physically.

When presenting, your physical comfort is very important, so again, take some time to try out various remotes before you commit. Also, these devices can be costly (some are $50 or more), so it's worth your while to experiment and decide carefully. A number of remotes are available at office supply stores and online.

The device I use to call a group back to order, for example, after a table discussion or other cooperative learning activity, is the Woodstock Percussion Zenergy Chime Solo Percussion Instrument. It's small (about seven inches long), cheap (less than $10), and travels well in its original box. When "dinged" with the mallet, the chime makes a noise that reverberates throughout the room. I found this item simply by searching using the word "chime" on Amazon.com. While I don't get kickbacks from Woodstock Percussion or Amazon, I'm happy to recommend that you set off on a search of your own for a product like this. I'm happy to report that the chime I chose has served me well for over two years of heavy travel, and it has never been criticized by participants in my staff development sessions.

As far as other advance purchases go, I recommend that you buy a pack of clear overhead transparencies and a large selection of Sharpie markers. Like me, you will most likely do a high number of presentations in school buildings. If there's one thing available in any school building, it's an overhead projector. If your computer dies, or if the projector dies, or if a hundred other things happen that may prevent you from using your beautifully designed PowerPoint presentation, be prepared to use an overhead and the transparencies and markers you've tucked inside your bag. If you have several colors of markers, you can sketch simple symbols and diagrams as you are speaking (in addition to words and phrases) to help your audience connect with your content. You can also model effective instructional strategies, like Cornell notes and cloze reading, if appropriate. When the technology goes down, it often creates a more relaxed and interactive environment—as long as you are prepared to "go with the flow" and proceed!

You may also want to consider a small, highly portable pair of external speakers (if you will use audio and/or video in your presentations) and one of the pocket-size camcorders (if you plan to shoot video of participant discussions, etc.). I personally do not use either of these items but have several colleagues who do, and they would not leave home without them. Because these items can also be costly, observe the techniques of other presenters in employing the tools. If you find you'd like to emulate their actions, investigate further and take time to comparison shop before committing.

> **Self-check: What could you do this week or this month to better prepare for the presentations you will make in the forthcoming year?**

Preparing *Before* the Presentation

You've most likely logged a great deal of time preparing the content and delivery of your presentation. However, on the day before it occurs, you must prepare all the materials you will need so that the presentation goes as smoothly as possible.

First, check all your equipment. Use address labels or other stickers to tag each piece of equipment you will have with you in the presentation room: laptop, power supply for the laptop, external speakers, remote slide advancer, books, etc. Every item is a potential lost item, and having your items clearly labeled increases the likelihood they will find their way back to you. You can also mark items with permanent marker if you don't have stickers.

Tip: I usually slip a page of address labels into the travel folder that I carry in my tote bag. If I buy a new book or other item during my trip, I have the labels right there, so I can stick one on the new item immediately. You could also slip a sheet of these into the back of a binder or notebook that you carry to your presentations. It's amazing how handy they become.

Make sure before you retire for the evening on the night prior to a presentation that you plug your laptop and cell phone in so that they charge fully. Also e-mail a backup copy of your presentation files to yourself or store them on an external server or website (like Google Docs or Wikispaces). Be aware, though, that if you have used a large number of photographic images, your files will be large and may be rejected by e-mail programs, external servers, and some file-sharing and storage websites. Check all the particulars long before you're ready to store your backup copies.

While you're charging your equipment and making backup copies, also store copies of your presentation and handouts on a jump drive, and put that jump drive into the bag you will carry the next day. By having copies in several locations, you can ensure that even if you drop your laptop and break it on the way to the presentation, there are other ways to actually give the presentation using the resources you carefully prepared.

If you are not carrying the copies of the handout you will use along with you to the site, it's a good idea to carry a copy of your handout (with your handwritten speaker's notes on it) plus a clean copy of your handout. If the copies weren't made yet or if they were not received or shipped for some reason, you have the master from which someone can make a new set. Go ahead the night before and print your copies of these very important documents; then tuck them into your bag for the next day.

Locate and replenish your speaker's emergency kit. In mine, I generally include the following: extra business cards; printout of my main contact's name and cell phone number and the address and phone number of the site; overhead transparencies, regular Sharpie markers for the transparencies, and fat, chisel-tip Sharpie markers for chart paper; spare pair of pantyhose; masking or painter's tape; safety pins; several Shout wipes; a travel-size can of Static Guard; extra batteries for my remote slide advancer; cough drops or hard candy; two bottles of water; a couple of teabags, several packets of Splenda, and several packets or a container of Coffee-mate; tissues or a handkerchief; Imodium, Gas-X, and a small bottle of pain reliever (like Aleve, Tylenol, or Advil). See the action steps at the end of this chapter and build your emergency kit well before your next engagement. You'll be prepared for lack of technology, wardrobe malfunctions, illness, and whatever else might come your way!

Timothy Koegel (2002), author of *The Exceptional Presenter*, recommends arriving at the presentation location an hour before the start time and splitting it forty-twenty, with the first forty minutes being spent preparing the room, equipment, handouts, etc. (p. 46). He says:

> Own the Room [sic]! You are responsible for the success or failure of the session. When the audience arrives, turn your undivided attention to meeting and greeting. Introduce audience members to one another. Be a conversation starter. (p. 46)

I agree with Koegel that it's up to me to do everything within my control to assure the success of the session. However, I always arrive forty-five minutes prior to the announced start time. I find that sometimes, especially if it's first thing in the morning, there is no one available an hour beforehand, even if my contact has told me that there would be. So instead of wasting fifteen minutes sitting in my car or knocking on a school door, watching for someone to arrive, I can spend that fifteen minutes having coffee, going through my presentation mentally, or reviewing my written notes in my hotel room one last time.

In the forty-five minutes or so prior to beginning, you will need to locate your room and get the technology up and running. If there is going to be a delay or problem with anything, it will be the technology!

If you have your own projector and laptop, make sure you have practiced linking the computer and projector together at home so you know which to start up first (each combination of the two machines seems to have its own requirements). If you have only a laptop, get it set up and linked to the site projector as soon as possible, and ask for assistance if necessary. If you have only a jump drive and are using the computer and projector available at the site, start up and move the necessary files and folders from the jump drive to the desktop of the computer. Then remove your jump drive and store it in your bag. Running the files from the computer instead of from the jump drive will speed up your presentation. (Just be sure to erase your files from the site computer's desktop at the end of the day.)

Aim to spend no more than twenty-five minutes getting the technology going and making the room "just right." You'll need to spend the twenty minutes just before your introduction welcoming participants and building your knowledge of their roles, experiences, successes, and concerns.

In order to make the room "just right," you'll need to make sure there is room for everyone to sit comfortably, push back their chairs, and place their belongings around them, all without blocking your access to any area of the room.

Walk to the back of the room and sit in several of the seats there. Can you see the screen and/or podium clearly? If not, move the tables and chairs, or ask someone to do this for you.

Walk the periphery of the room. Are there any cords or other items that may cause someone to trip or stumble? Use the masking tape in your emergency kit to repair these, or ask someone to fix the problem. Are all necessary supplies accessible to the participants? If not, ask your contact person to help.

Find the closest restrooms. Find the closest exit doors. Commit these to memory.

As people start to enter, usually about twenty minutes beforehand, you should be wholly focused on making connections and building relationships. Stop moving furniture! Greet each person. Shake hands and introduce yourself. Ask what their roles are and *really listen*. Ask a genuine question and show your interest in the answer.

Make mental notes about how you can take what these folks tell you and put it right into your presentation. For example, "Linda mentioned to me this morning that she finds it hard as a team leader to get the members of the team to all contribute their ideas during the collaboration time. If you, too, experience that problem, you'll find several specific techniques today to try at that next meeting. They worked for me when I was a team leader last year, and I bet you can use them or adapt them so they work for you and your team, too."

About a minute before you're introduced, stop moving and breathe deeply, from the diaphragm. (An excellent article on deep breathing appears at http://health.discovery.com/centers/althealth/deepbreath/deepbreathe.html.) A few deep breaths will do wonders to calm you down and will also assist you in having a louder, clearer voice.

> ***Self-check:** In what type of venues will you be making your next few presentations? What's most important to remember about those settings so that the learning is maximized?*

Being Prepared *During* the Presentation

Being prepared during the session is critical. If you did audience mapping in the early preparation stages, then you know your attendees well and have already given thought to their pressing needs and possible forms of resistance. You'll need to maintain your composure at all times, so think through how you will respond to difficult questions and difficult people. If you are truly prepared and have confidence in your knowledge and in your ability to handle tricky situations, you will do well during your presentation, no matter what!

What follows is a list of certain scenarios and suggestions for handling them. These scenarios represent my own experiences over the past five years, plus the experiences of some of my respected colleagues at The Leadership and Learning Center. Collectively, the examples represent a decade of presentations and presenters who give more than a hundred presentations per year. While some examples may seem unbelievable to you, trust me—they are real!

1. *Low attendance.* If presenting at conferences or other "voluntary attendance" venues, the possibility exists that very few people will show. My boss, colleague, and friend Doug Reeves fondly tells the story of an education conference about a decade ago at which he presented. His session was scheduled in a typical, large, poorly lit, ballroom-type setting, and only seven people attended. When he realized, only a few minutes before he was to start, that the 100+ people he had

prepared for were not coming, he just said to himself, "Well, these are the right folks to be here, so let's go with it."

Instead of standing at the podium and presenting in the formal manner he had planned, he sat with the seven people, had an informal conversation, and allowed them to ask a lot of questions and share their own experiences. This group of seven people indeed turned out to be exactly the right people to be there, as several long-lasting consulting relationships resulted.

The moral of this story? Adjust your methods when necessary, but give every group your all. You'll be rewarded, and they will learn something. I'm reminded that Nancy Duarte (2008) often says that every presentation is high stakes and every audience deserves the absolute best (p. xix).

2. *High attendance.* You may experience times when your session literally overflows. Obviously, you should work with your facilitator and building staff to ensure there are chairs for everyone; no one should sit on the floor, even in the most crowded circumstances at any conference. It simply won't help a person learn!

Also do your best to start on time, even though people may still be shuffling around, getting settled, and so forth. Acknowledge in your opening remarks that the room is overcrowded but that you are determined to make the best of the situation.

Decide quickly whether or not you have to adjust the directions for activities you had planned, and if you must, tell the audience up front. For example, I had to say to a room of two hundred one time, "I had planned several cooperative learning tasks for us today that also involved movement. Now that we are crammed in here as we are, I'm probably going to substitute elbow-to-elbow pairs and knee-to-knee triads instead. Of course, if you prefer to do any of these activities individually through some silent or written reflection, please do! The important thing to remember is to engage with the material as best we can in the situation in which we find ourselves, and don't hesitate to pass a note to me or talk with me at our break if you have a suggestion that can help our group work together more productively."

3. *Your computer doesn't work.* In this situation, it's best if you arrived forty-five minutes prior to the beginning of the presentation, because you have several options to exercise (and time to exercise them). You can ask your facilitator or the building contact person to find you another computer (often there will be one in the room that is dedicated to presentations). If you have your presentation on a jump drive, as I've recommended, any machine will do.

If another machine is not available, or doesn't arrive in time, go ahead and start your presentation, using your hard-copy printout as your guide. Ask for an overhead projector and use the transparencies and markers you have in your emergency kit. No emergency kit? Ask for the supplies. Direct people to their handouts, if you are using handouts, and utilize the overhead, whiteboard, chart paper, chalkboard, or even the walls—whatever is available.

If you have only walls, ask for someone to bring you poster paper (or bulletin board paper), and attach it to the walls to serve as your writing surface. You should have masking tape and markers in your emergency kit.

And what if the handouts are missing, there is no computer or overhead, there is no chart paper, and it's just you and your audience? Well, this is where all the practicing you did comes into play—it's you and them! You have your voice, your gestures, your movements, your enthusiasm, and your knowledge. And they have ears and eyes. So make it happen!

4. *The projector doesn't work.* If you do have a computer that is working properly but no way to display your presentation, go ahead and display your presentation for only you to see, and proceed, using the slides that only you see to guide your work.

If you have a small group, let's say ten or fewer, then you can even display your presentation from your computer screen for them to see, as the size of the display won't be too small.

If allowing the participants to see your screen is not feasible, or if the group is too large, simply work from the handouts. Now, your handouts should *not* contain a copy of the slides, but they probably do have some of the most important points of your content highlighted. So use your notes (that no one can see) and teach the content, guiding your audience through it, using conversation, activities, and your shining personality to communicate the big idea and key points.

5. *Your remote slide advancer (clicker) doesn't work.* This is an easy problem to handle. First, ask the facilitator if you can borrow one. If you can't, you will simply need to position yourself close to your computer keyboard when it's necessary to flip a slide.

At times when you have to advance rapidly, you will need to stay close to your keyboard. Just remember not to seem tied to the computer; stand to one side of it sometimes, and alternate with the other side. If you are presenting in a large venue like a ballroom or auditorium with a stage, you may want to ask the facilitator to sit at your keyboard and advance for you when you give an unobtrusive signal, like a nod or the word phrase "next please." If you start out with another person advancing for you, and it's not working well, you can always let the person off the hook at the next scheduled break and take over yourself.

6. *The room becomes too warm or too cold.* This is a tricky situation. Most schools, hotels, and convention centers have rooms that are hard to regulate. In any presentation, you may be warm yourself, because, of all the people in the room, you are probably the most animated, active, and possibly, nervous. Therefore, it's hard to judge whether others are warm, too. So look for the signs: droopy

eyelids, fanning, drinking water, removing sweaters and jackets. If you notice these signs, you probably need to ask your host to see if the room can be cooled. An ideal temperature range is 69 to 72 degrees. Most audiences will be comfortable in that range.

If you have a choice, go cooler, not warmer. Cooler is easier to deal with. You can always get people up and moving; just throw in a standing pair-share activity and force folks to partner with someone from the opposite side of the room or from a different table than theirs.

Rooms cooler than 66 degrees are highly uncomfortable for most audiences, though, so do all you can to reduce the likelihood of a temperature in that range. If your host cannot arrange for the settings to be changed, during a break or even an extended cooperative learning activity, step out into the hall and look for anyone who appears to be part of the custodial or maintenance staff. Generally these folks will be more than happy to assist you. In a hotel or conference facility, ask anyone who's carrying a radio, or specifically ask for the conference/convention manager.

7. *The electricity goes out.* I have had had this experience twice—once, for a period of about twenty minutes in the middle of a day-long session, and in the other instance, at the very end of a three-day train-the-trainer program. This time, power didn't come back on, and the room quickly reached about 80 degrees.

So how to handle the lack of electricity if it occurs? Safety first! Ensure everyone stays seated while you or your host checks with someone else in the building to see why this may have happened. If there are several laptops in the room, they will continue to display until their batteries run down, so this will provide light. Cell phones can also function as flashlights. You should continue presenting and ask one person per table to shine their cell phone or laptop toward the others so there is enough light to see you and, if possible, also to read the handout.

Generally a lack of power is resolved in less than thirty minutes. You don't want to give people a break, because it's dangerous for them to be up and moving if the room is indeed very dark. In the case of a building failure, then the hallways may be dark, also, and it's best for everyone just to stay put.

On the day the power went out in my train-the-trainer session, we carefully formed a circle, with me holding my laptop, facing them, to finish the material. This was a group of twenty, and they could see my screen and also my face, just above the screen. There was a tiny bit of light coming from the door in the hallway, which opened to the outside. Our air conditioning was off, too, obviously, and within fifteen minutes, the room was very stuffy. After about twenty minutes, someone from the building's office came and told us that they had been in contact with the local power company, and the power would be off indefinitely. Thank goodness we were at the last thirty minutes or so of our last day, so we quickly closed our discussion and left.

8. *The sound from the presentation next door is competing with you/your sound.* This is a fairly common occurrence, especially in convention-type settings. Again, the first thing to do is to look to your host or facilitator. This person can leave the room and check on the situation while you continue to hold the attention of your audience.

Never stop presenting! If the sound totally overpowers your voice, change your presentation strategy and have participants silently skim through your entire handout or read a short text related to your topic that you quickly display on the screen. Then have them conduct small group discussions. If you can orchestrate an activity like this for about ten minutes, then your host should be able to get the problem solved.

If it's still not solved in that amount of time, you will need to continue to improvise. One time I took my entire group (about twenty people) out in the hallway and taught as if we were in a football huddle. This took about fifteen minutes; I finished some content I had been presenting and then described an activity I wanted them to do when we got back in the room. We re-entered the room, they set off to work, and the problem was resolved in about fifteen more minutes. We actually moved to another room because the hotel staff couldn't figure out how to prevent my next-door neighbor's audio from being piped into my room.

9. *The landscaping crew is mowing or blowing leaves right outside your window, or the maintenance crew is pressure-washing the building, or the parking lot is being repaved (and other variations of annoying industrial noises).* I am a magnet for lawnmowers and leaf-blowers. Between March and September, I usually tell my audiences that I'm sure at some point, someone will be cutting grass or blowing leaves right outside our window or door. More than two-thirds of the time, my prediction is dead-on. I happen to have been a high school administrator and am therefore blessed with a loud voice that I can crank up even louder. So usually the outside noise is not a problem.

However, if you are soft-spoken, or if it's uncomfortable for you physically to raise your voice, consider asking for a microphone and speaker system at every engagement at which you plan to be working with more than thirty people. If you have a microphone handy, any loud, external noise can be handled without you having to strain your voice. If you always travel by car to your speaking engagements, you may even consider buying your own voice amplification apparatus and keeping it with you so you can dash out and get it if you must.

10. *You trip, stumble, fall off the stage, or otherwise lose your footing.* First, if you're really injured, say so, and ask for help. I've had colleagues who have fallen and have suffered broken toes, concussions, and worse. If you're presenting in a school, generally a school nurse can come to your aid. If not, someone needs to call 911 immediately.

If you're not injured seriously, do your best not to get ruffled. Obviously you will be embarrassed, but remember that most everyone in the room will be concerned for your well-being. Get up, dust yourself off, and do the best you can. Or sit in a chair and present for a while until you gain your composure. I'm notorious for stumbling over extension cords, and I take great care to practice walking the room, gesturing, and moving around in the forty-five minutes I have when I arrive before I begin speaking. I have stumbled over cords before, and I just laugh at myself and tell the audience, "When I was a classroom teacher, I did that at least twice a week! Thank you for being nicer to me when I just now did it than my high school students often were!"

11. *A video or sound clip doesn't work properly.* This is a very common problem. I attended a national conference just a month ago and saw a video clip played without sound—and the presenter was one of the most famous, internationally respected educational researchers there is. If it can happen to him, it can happen to you!

Again, I'll repeat my mantra from another chapter: practice makes perfect. Practice running the clip over and over again prior to your session, and certainly try it again as you are setting up and readying your technology. Even if you've done all that, you can still experience a frozen screen, muffled sound, or other problems. My rule is that I don't use video or audio to make a critical point; I use them only to support a point, or to send the audience to a break, or to make them laugh. In this way, if the clip malfunctions, I'm not flustered, and the point can still be made effectively.

12. *Someone acts hostile toward you.* I hope you never have happen to you what I had happen to me in a high school during a meeting with only twelve teachers in a small conference room. An angry male teacher got up out of his seat and approached me, waving his finger at me, yelling! I thought it was a role-play at first, but it was not. He was angry, and he was physically intimidating to me. I had to remember all my de-escalating behaviors from administrator training: I breathed deeply, maintained eye contact, and took a step back, trying to widen the space between us. I nodded and remained calm, and amazingly, he finished his rant and turned to go back to his seat as his principal was entering the room. She knew nothing of what had just happened but sat down, as the rest of the teachers just stared at me, aghast. I took another deep breath, and did the best I could to summarize what I think his complaint really was—that the world outside the school was violent and dangerous, and that the teachers had limited influence. (A recent graduate had been killed in drive-by shooting a few days prior, and a current student had been arrested.)

I said something like the following: "I understand that there are forces that are competing with academics. I'm sure all of you are saddened and perhaps even angered by the recent shooting that occurred only a block away, and I'm so sorry that you've lost a young man that many of you knew and taught. It does seem that in education, sometimes, there's only so much impact we can have against all the other odds. But I also know that good teachers *save* kids. Good teachers can offer troubled kids a way out of all the mess that they perceive their lives to be . . ."

I've encountered other, less physically hostile situations, too, but they are all unsettling. If an audience member asks a hostile question or makes an inappropriate comment, first of all, be quiet and *breathe*. As the person is stating a complaint or asking a question, force yourself to breathe deeply and calmly. Do your best not only to listen but to deconstruct why this person may be behaving as such.

As Garr Reynolds says, when audience members ask questions or give comments, you should be gracious; even if someone is being difficult, you must keep to the high ground and at all times, and as a true professional, remain cool and in control. Reynolds goes on to remind us that it is one's reputation at stake, so it behooves you to be gracious even with the most challenging of audiences (http://www.garrreynolds.com/Presentation/delivery.html).

I would add to his sage advice by providing this analysis: if someone is being difficult or disrespectful, *it's not about you*. Don't take it personally. Try to figure out what is behind the comment or question. Is the person grieving over something, as perhaps the man I described earlier was? Does the person feel incompetent? Is the person scared of trying something new? Is the person already competent at a skill you are discussing and is feeling disrespected? Does the person have a nasty boss? Is the person suffering in his or her personal life? Listen with empathy first and for content second. You do have to address the content once the person is finished, but you really need to address the feeling tone of the comment more than the content. In these situations, you have to do two things: *show empathy first and regain control second.*

You are in charge of the presentation; never forget that! If the person persists, or interrupts, or again becomes hostile, take control. Ask the person to leave the room if you must (I have done this successfully at least two times that I recall). The other attendees will appreciate your assertiveness and your keeping the presentation on track.

13. *You have an overly chatty person*. It's funny how teachers enforce silence in their classrooms, but when they are in staff development sessions, they can be the chattiest people in the world. The chatty attendee presents you with quite a challenge. You may want to give a whole-group reminder once, early on in the session, when you notice some chatter. In this way, you're not singling anyone out.

However, after giving one whole-group reminder of the norms, don't continue to do this. It becomes obvious after one such reminder just who the violator is, and other audience members will resent your not handling the situation effectively if you continue to be vague. If the person continues to talk, you might just pause when you notice it happening, and become silent yourself. Being silent will draw everyone's attention to you, except perhaps for the talkative person, who will eventually realize he or she is the only one not looking at you, waiting to hear your very next word. Sometimes loquacious folks will talk during the times when another audience member is asking a question; this is the ultimate in rudeness, I think, so usually I just maintain eye contact with the person who is directing a question to me and say, sometimes repeatedly, "I'm sorry. I'm having trouble hearing you." This usually prompts someone seated near the offender to call their attention to the discussion at hand.

As a last resort, you can speak with a chatty person privately—and do ensure that no one else hears you. Simply pull the person aside, and start with something like this: "I noticed that you're talking a bit while I'm presenting, and I'm not sure if that means you're actively processing the content or if you're bored or frustrated." Then allow the person to respond. The person who means no harm will apologize and change her behavior. The person who is trying to sabotage you will let you know, and at that point, you can invite that person to leave the session and instead do something else that will be more personally useful for them (and thus, less stressful for you).

14. *You or someone else becomes suddenly and violently ill*. Any sudden, violent illness should first be handled with a fifteen-minute break. In that time, you can assess whether or not you can continue, or in the case of an ill attendee, you can rustle up the necessary assistance.

If you are the person who falls ill, seek out your host or facilitator first, and if possible, discuss what alternatives might be available in the case you can't continue to present. Could you do the session on another day? Can someone (there in the room or quickly available) step in and finish for you? Use your best problem-solving skills, and don't hesitate to have someone call 911 if it's warranted.

15. *There is an emergency like a fire, fire drill, bomb scare, etc.* Again, handle the emergency as you would have in your classroom. Follow the directions of the person or people in charge. Never lose your cool. Be patient and resume the presentation when the scare is over, if it is indeed over in time for you to continue, and if people seem emotionally able to attend to your presentation.

If the emergency event goes on past your end time, or if the people in charge cancel your presentation, then you will have to reschedule. If the scare is over quickly but people seem incredibly uptight, propose a thirty-minute break and ask the audience to take care of all their personal needs during that time and to return, ready to pay full attention to the content you will share. They can always choose to leave during that thirty-minute window if there is a need for them to do so. You are merely providing the out while also trying to move forward and do what you were asked to do.

16. *You lose your voice.* This is an incredibly tough situation. If you're able to speak in a whisper, ask for a microphone and continue to present, using a whisper but also using the microphone.

If it's incredibly painful for you to continue talking, or if you can't even muster a whisper, you can offer to copy and share the notes you have for the next section of material with the participants. You could also opt to print the notes-page layout of all your remaining PowerPoint slides and to "jigsaw" this content—only if you feel the notes you have recorded there are truly helpful to the participants. If you wrote out an entire script during the practice phase, then your notes might be very helpful to the attendees. If you have only skeletal notes, because you have practiced so much that you have truly internalized your presentation, then your notes may be of no use at all to the audience.

Without a voice, you will have to determine the best course. It is always best not to cancel once you have started, so whatever you can do to avoid that is recommended. Using amplified whispers, handing out your notes, utilizing any video files you may have that are on your topic, or orchestrating the reading of professional literature on your topic are all ways you can adapt to the loss of your voice.

> ***Self-check:** Think of a time you saw one of the previous scenarios (or a similar scenario) occur in a professional learning session. How was it handled? How did you feel after the situation was handled?*

Being Prepared *After* the Presentation

The presentation is not really over when you have stopped presenting. People will hang around to chat with each other and/or with you. Your host may want to have a conversation with you. You have to straighten the room and deal with the people who are demanding your attention. The tips that follow are intended to help you make the few minutes after you finish speaking less hectic for you.

1. *Avoid the paper shuffle.* At the last break prior to the dismissal of your attendees, put all the required items on their tables. This includes any forms that must be completed for them to receive pay or credit, evaluation forms about the session, and your business cards. Make sure you stop about ten minutes prior to the announced ending time and call their attention to these items.

2. *Always end early.* No one has ever rushed up to me to tell me they thought my presentation was too short and that I should call the group back and continue. Everyone sees five little minutes as a gift, and they will be in much better spirits as they complete the evaluation forms if you give them that gift. Stopping five or ten minutes early—and I don't recommend more than fifteen minutes—shows that you respect the time and needs of your participants. Five to fifteen minutes allow them to complete their paper work, pack up their belongings, say good-bye to a few colleagues, and still be out the door at the announced ending time.
3. *You forget something.* This is inevitable; you just don't want it to be a chronic problem. If you have attached address labels to your items, then you can call your host or facilitator later and ask that the article be sent to you postage-due. If you forget an item that is not tagged, your first step should be to call your host or the person in charge of the venue. Hotel housekeeping and banquet staff are usually quite adept at logging items into their lost and found systems quickly.
4. *People line up to ask questions.* This situation is similar to parent-teacher conference night: those folks who don't really need to see you for the answers to a burning question will be exactly the ones who want to speak with you. Quickly survey the line and the faces, and deal with each person as promptly and as courteously as possible, all the while gathering your books, markers, cords, and the like.

    If someone else is using the room right after you, you'll have a very small window of time to clean up and get out, and you still must deal with the folks who want to talk with you—so you must be a master of both courtesy and multi-tasking. If a person's question is too detailed to handle quickly, take the person's card or note their e-mail address, and e-mail them later that evening to follow up.
5. *You need a ride.* Perhaps you're heading somewhere you need to be quickly and someone brought you to the place where you just completed your presentation. If you forgot to get your transportation worked out before the presentation began and now your need is desperate, check with a member of the banquet staff (in a hotel setting) or the school secretary (in a school setting) ASAP after your presentation ends. These folks will be able to assist you.

Action Steps

1. Make an "emergency kit" to take to your next presentation. At minimum, include the following items: hard copy of your contact's name and cell num-

ber; the site's location, physical address, and phone number; masking tape, several chart markers, one bottle of water (that can be refilled as the day goes on). Brainstorm other items you may need to include.
2. List the items you are considering purchasing as a result of reading this chapter.
3. Think of other presenters whom you admire for their preparedness and skilled delivery. List them. If possible, e-mail or call at least two people on your list in the next month. Ask if you can come sit in on one of their presentations or, at the very least, discuss with them how they prepare for the excellent delivery that you have seen them provide.
4. Review the handout I often use with teachers I train to deliver some of my company's seminars, below.

Angela's General Tips for Presenters

- Make sure you have the PowerPoint presentation saved on your computer and also on a jump drive. That way, if there is a problem with the computer, you have a backup copy.
- Print a hard copy of the PowerPoint presentation and have it available to you *at all times* during the presentation—just in case you need it.
- Wear comfortable shoes! Also, for large groups (over thirty), wear clothing on which it's possible to attach a lapel microphone. You may need this (and you should make sure your on-site setup person knows this in advance).
- Always be on-site at least forty-five minutes before the scheduled starting time. You'll probably need to rearrange furniture, check the equipment, and, of course, greet your "students."
- If possible, have some kind of "welcoming" or "tone-setting" poster or sign displayed as participants enter. Or have some picturesque PowerPoint slides running to get their minds geared up for the learning. Have their materials already placed on the tables if possible; this will save time later.
- Bring your own chart markers, blank overhead transparencies, overhead markers, and masking tape. You never know when you might need one or more of these items.
- Bring two bottles of water. You will need them! You may also want to have mints or cough drops handy in case of an unexpected scratchy throat.
- If co-presenting, determine signals or code words you will have for each other beforehand. Helpful signals include those meaning "we need to move on" and "I would like to jump in now."
- Do not turn your back to the audience when writing on chart paper or board. If you must turn, be as quick as possible! Also, do not face the screen

and speak toward it. Always speak to your audience and look at them. Be careful not to step between the projector and screen when speaking. Stand to the side or circulate so that you don't have a weird light show playing on your torso.

- Be careful with Post-It chart paper pads. The sheets will stick to each other on the chart stand when you flip them back after using them. *Carefully* peel each sheet back after you use it and flatten it completely.
- When using PowerPoint, hit the letter B to black out the screen. Hit it again to bring the slide back up. You must be in slide show view for this to work. Remember: Hit B to black it out; hit B to bring it back.
- Invest in a remote control slide advancer or ask that your setup person provide one for you so that no one has to click through the slide show from the computer keyboard. Having a remote allows you to circulate freely.

CHAPTER FIVE

Practice Makes Perfect

You've gotten into your audience's shoes, you've crafted your core message, and you've designed a visually powerful presentation plus accompanying hard-copy material. Now it's time to commit yourself to your performance.

If you followed the advice given at the end of chapter 3, you have reduced your slides down to their essence. You have practiced what you will say, at least a couple of times. Now you must learn to perform—to deliver your story to its intended audience—so that the big idea resonates with them when you are done.

In this chapter, you will refine your narration, practice the final draft of your presentation, and plan very specifically for what will happen from the moment the audience turns their attention to you.

Finalize the Script

You should have a final (or almost-final) draft of your slides if you have followed the recommended process thus far. Now is the time to make final tweaks.

Ask yourself the following as you click through your slides one last time, and make adjustments as needed:

- Are the audience's needs the basis for the presentation? How is this evident?
- Is the big idea obvious?
- Do all key points support that big idea?
- Is an organizational structure apparent?
- Do colors, backgrounds, fonts, and other design elements work in harmony? Does everything look "just right"?
- Is text limited *only* to what is essential?

- Do all visuals (photos, data displays, symbols, icons, etc.) clarify and enhance the message?
- Do animations and/or transitions deepen meaning rather than distract?

Dress Rehearsal

Nancy Duarte (2008) asserts that the biggest issue facing presenters today is that they don't take time to rehearse (p. 220). The PowerPoint program, as it is often applied, coaxes us into not rehearsing. If we fall for the seduction of the bulleted templates and use copious amounts of text on each slide, we can use the text as a crutch. It's easier not to devote time to rehearsing when you know you can look at a slide and see almost everything you would say anyway right there in front of you.

However, you have now gone through a thinking and designing process that has encouraged you to strip your ideas down to their bare essences and to make a strong, emotional connection to your audience through words and visuals. It won't be good enough to stand in front of your audience and dispassionately read from your notes. Instead, you must be the consummate performer. In order for your ideas to be understood and your call to action to be internalized, you must be the best presenter you can be—part actor, part teacher, and part salesperson.

Take your script one last time and present it to yourself, alone in an empty room, as you click through your slides. Or, if you prefer, present to a pet or a member of your family.

Warning: family members grow bored quickly, whereas a cat perched in a sunny spot usually does not! Cats and dogs make terrific audiences because they won't criticize you one bit.

Another option is to do what Nancy Duarte sometimes does—post pictures of the faces of people you know on the wall, and present to them as if they are real (http://blog.duarte.com/2008/07/tips-for-remote-presenters). This type of run-through can help you with eye contact, gestures, and movement if you place the "people" in a setup that mimics real conditions.

Don't underestimate the rehearsals. You must talk through your presentation, *out loud* (not just in your head), *over and over again* before delivering it live.

If you do not practice "live," you risk many potential negatives. You may forget to share important material. You might fumble through certain parts because you are unsure of what to say. You don't drive one of your key points home as well as possible, perhaps, or you forget your sequencing. You could draw a total blank when you see a slide with only a visual image and no text. You may speed through material and run out of things to say before time is up.

Do this last run-through mirroring authentic conditions as closely as possible. Say every word you plan to say. Record yourself one last time if you wish. You will thank yourself a dozen times over if you put this last bit of "elbow grease" into your delivery—and your audience will benefit tremendously from your thoughtful, thorough preparation.

Appearance

As you are getting ready to meet the folks you will be teaching, take great care to appear as professional and knowledgeable as possible, yet also approachable.

One guideline that's helpful is to be just one level dressier than most of the audience members will be, so if you are working with teachers, a blazer is necessary for men (although a necktie may not be), and a businesslike dress, skirt, or pants are necessary for women (although a matched suit may not be in order). If your audience includes a healthy representation of administrators, or consists of all administrators, a suit and tie is best for men, and a suit (with skirt or pants) is best for women.

Women, please be aware of your accessories and jewelry. I have been to presentations during which I was very distracted by the jangling of someone's bracelet. Neckwear (scarves, large necklaces) can interfere with a lapel microphone. I'm not being sexist here; men could certainly have accessories that interfere with delivery, but I've just never seen it.

Another thing to be aware of is cologne. Some folks have sensitivities or allergies to chemicals found in perfumes, men's colognes, and scents from antiperspirants and lotions. If you are one to slather on scents, realize that you may actually destroy someone's learning. I myself get severe headaches after exposed to strong scents. If I were attending your session, and you were within a couple of feet of me at any time, I would probably have to get up and leave to ensure I could have a productive day and not be bedridden from a migraine.

Recently, I did several presentations for large audiences (four hundred–plus) in Newfoundland, Canada. The speakers who opened each morning's general session and welcomed the other speakers were so considerate of health and nutrition concerns. They reminded everyone that we were in close quarters and should be mindful of any products we used that might offend someone else's sensibilities. They urged us (gently) to cover our coughs and sneezes properly and to use the hand sanitizer that seemed to be supplied everywhere—it was in the restrooms, could be found in dispensers on the walls, and was supplied to participants in travel-size bottles to carry with them.

They also pointed out all the "nutrition breaks" that were on our agenda and the "nutrition areas" that were in various locations. Water, coffee, tea, and healthy snacks were abundant. It was absolutely the most humane conference schedule and most polite group of folks that I have ever seen!

Another noticeable feature: *I didn't hear a cell phone ring even once when were in any of the sessions!* Sadly, a cell phone ring has interrupted the last two Broadway shows I've seen. We could learn much from our Canadian neighbors.

In summary:

- Don't wear anything that could make someone else uncomfortable.
- Don't spread your germs.
- Take care of your needs for water and food so that you feel your best and are prepared for learning.
- Make and take your phone calls at another time.

Keep in mind that a presenter's makeup, hairstyle, clothing, and manners (like whether or not they are seen sneezing and then shaking someone's hand, or whether they are seen yakking on their cell phone in the presence of others) convey a great deal of information to audience members. Once you are on-site and are preparing for your presentation, every nuance of your appearance and demeanor is on display. Be mindful.

> **Self-check: What might I have in my wardrobe and my grooming routine that I should consider changing? Why?**

Does Someone Speak Before You Speak?

In many cases, you will be introduced by someone else. Do your best to control the quality, length, and nonverbal tones of this introduction as best you can. Sometimes you won't know who's introducing you to the crowd until minutes beforehand (for example, at a national conference). In this case, you'll have to quickly assess what the person plans to say and make a snap judgment about the person's speaking talents. In other cases, the person will contact you ahead of time and ask what you would like said. This is ideal! In yet other cases, the introductory speaker will simply look you up via the Internet and cobble something together.

Whatever the situation, exert as much control on your introduction as possible. First impressions speak volumes, and your introduction forces people to look at you and to begin forming their opinions of you.

Let's walk through each of the aforementioned scenarios.

A common one is the one in which you arrive at your presentation room in a convention facility or hotel, forty-five minutes prior to your talk (only if someone is not presenting there before you are). You start setting up, and twenty minutes or so later, attendees start to arrive.

About ten minutes before your announced start time, someone rushes in, introduces themselves, and says, "I'll be introducing you. What would you like me to say?" What's even worse is if the person says, "I'll be introducing you. I thought I would just read the bio that you provided to the committee." In the worse of the two situations, emphatically say, "Oh, please don't. That bio is so dry! Do you mind if I give you a couple of things to say instead?" Be prepared to provide a couple of important and memorable tidbits immediately.

In the case of the cobbled-together, Google-search introduction, peruse what the person found. It could be totally acceptable. If it's too lengthy (meaning it would take more than a minute or two), suggest some revisions. If there are items you would like to remove, simply ask if you may.

And lastly, if someone contacts you well ahead of your presentation and asks what you would like your introduction to consist of, be prepared to provide two or three of your most meaningful professional accomplishments, something personal but not too personal, and some context about where you live, how long you've been in education, and/or what some of your interests or passions are.

For example, I usually ask people introducing me to say that I'm from one of the most beautiful small towns in America, Beaufort, South Carolina, the location where much of the movie *Forrest Gump* was filmed. I tell them that I have three well-loved Labrador retrievers and cat (plus a terrific husband, too). And as for my professional life, I'm a senior professional development associate at The Leadership and Learning Center. Prior to that role, I had over fifteen years experience as a classroom teacher, instructional coach, and building administrator. Lastly, I am an active educational researcher and writer, having published three books and many training manuals and other educational materials.

> ***Self-check:** What information would you like for others to include when introducing you? How, exactly, would you like them to say it? Draft an appropriate introduction.*

Off to a Good Start

Rick Altman says to remember that *you* are the presentation; your slides are not (Oct. 24, 2008, http://betterppt.typepad.com/betterpresentingcom/2008/10/index.html). When it's time for you to begin speaking, that's an important piece of advice to take to heart.

Take Altman's advice and create a home base where you place your notes, water, and other items you might need. Spread all your notes across the table so you can see them quickly if you step over there. They can also be good resources for you as you take questions (you can peek at your notes if need be).

On the computer you are using, which functions as your "dashboard," have all the files you might access during the presentation open and minimized before you begin. You will not create unnecessary delays searching for files in response to an audience member's question or to an idea you have as you speak if you take this important step first.

Ensure that the lighting allows your audience members to see both you and your slides. *Don't ever put yourself in the dark.* You are the value-added piece; the participants cannot understand the slides without your teaching!

If darkness will enhance the beauty of your slide show, then turn the lights down, but use a separate lamp or spotlight near you, so that your audience can see you clearly at all times. Rick Altman (2007) also recommends that when you are standing near the screen and are referring to it closely, you stand facing your audience to their left because this is the position where they start reading—from left to right (p. 146).

Seth Godin (2001) reminds us:

> When you show up to give a presentation, people want to use both parts of their brain. So they use the right side to judge the way you talk, the way you dress and your body language. Often, people come to a conclusion about your presentation by the time you're on the second slide. After that, it's often too late for your bullet points to do you much good. (no page number)

Timothy Koegel (2002) echoes Godin when he shares that 55 percent of our speaking impact is determined nonverbally—through appearance, posture, gestures, eye contact, and body language, including our facial expressions (p. 21). As you begin, be very conscious of these factors.

Right before speaking, put those shoulders back, and smile warmly, even if you feel nervous. Take a moment to be silent and allow all eyes and attention to be on you after you are introduced. In other words, show that you "own" the room.

Then, control the pace of your speaking. Many of us speak more quickly than normal when we are nervous, so if you are one who speaks rapidly anyway, you need to tell yourself to slow down.

Avoid the most common error of people on loudspeakers everywhere and enunciate! Saying *every* syllable of *every* word clearly and deliberately enhances the comprehension of your audience members. If necessary, repeat key words and phrases and again, enunciate.

Use hand gestures and other movements deliberately. For example, when you reference data that describe an increase, raise your hand to simulate the increase. Do the opposite for a decrease. Koegel also reminds us that most people will forget 95 percent of what you say within minutes of hearing it (p. 34), so being as dramatic as possible helps your big idea take hold.

As you begin your presentation, control your words, control your body language, and let your passion shine through!

Coasting Along

As you continue your presentation, remain aware of your gestures, expressions, and movements. As Garr Reynolds (2008) says, "be fully present at that moment in time. . . . It is impossible to have a truly successful presentation when you are 'somewhere else'" (p. 185).

In the time that you have with your audience, you must offer them something of value that addresses their pressing needs. In order to do this well, you must constantly monitor what you are saying and doing in addition to monitoring the audience's responses. Keeping fully focused on the here and now during a presentation is essential.

Remember, too, that you are performing. Do what you must do to keep your audience's attention. Move around, speak more dramatically, involve people, black out the screen when you want all eyes on you. Put yourself out there, connect with your audience, and bring your information to life.

Use humor as the opportunity arises, *but don't use sarcasm*. Audiences will remember a sarcastic comment or gesture far longer than they will remember the substance of your talk.

Also avoid telling jokes. This is always a risky maneuver—you could forget the punch line, you could offend someone, or you could appear arrogant. The best kind of humor is self-deprecating humor.

Resist the urge that some speakers have to either stand rock-hard in one position or to do the complete opposite, pace to and fro incessantly. Avoid a lectern. Circulate, but don't pace. Stand still, slow down, and repeat key words or phrases for emphasis. Make every word and every motion count.

Keep the energy high during your presentation. Even in a keynote with hundreds of people present, you can call on people (with the help of another person and a handheld microphone), assign quick table-talk activities, and intersperse writing and talking throughout the presentation. A variety of quiet times and interactive times helps the audience stay energized.

Cliff Atkinson (2008) sums good delivery up well when he says, "With the screen behind the speaker, the audience sees and quickly digests the slide and then pays attention to the speaker and his or her verbal explanation. The entire experience appears seamless to the audience" (p. 42). Create the seamless, meaningful presentation that clearly sets you apart from other presenters.

> *Self-check: Where do I usually stand in a presentation? Do I move enough throughout the room, covering all areas and not just those that I favor or feel safe in? How can I weave various types of activities throughout my session to keep the audience engaged?*

Handling Questions

Whether you handle questions as they arise in your session or only at times that you have determined, you must handle them deftly. In order to do so, you must listen carefully and respond in a manner that will impart information but also honor the person asking the question.

Learn to paraphrase well; this is a vital skill for presenters. As single participants or groups offer comments or work on an activity in your workshop, stop to paraphrase often.

Robert Garmston (2006) gives this helpful advice to staff developers about paraphrasing:

- Summarize what you hear (from one person or several) and then ask, "Does this seem a fair statement about where you are?"
- Avoid beginning with "I think I hear you saying." This is dated and annoying.
- Use the pronoun "you" when you begin speaking. For example, "You are wondering" or "You're pleased with."
- Show tentativeness by raising your voice slightly at the end of your paraphrase, inviting listeners to chime in to correct or clarify.
- Be succinct. The paraphrase shouldn't be long enough that you need to stop speaking to take a breath.
- Don't paraphrase too often—only when you sense the group could benefit. Paraphrasing too often is an inexperienced presenter's error.

After either simply repeating a person's question or paraphrasing, it's then time to answer the question. Don't pretend you know an answer when you don't. It's far better to say, "I'm not sure I can give you a complete answer about that right now, but I'd be happy to correspond with you after the presentation."

Some questions are designed to force you to express a strongly held opinion. Don't fall for this trick! If a participant poses a question that generates heat on each side of the debate, make sure you give reasoned, unbiased summaries of each side if possible. If you give a one-sided response, you risk alienating part of your audience.

The best way to prepare for a question-and-answer session is to know your material deeply. *Rest assured that you know more about the topic than anyone else in the room does.* You have thoughtfully studied and prepared a dynamite presentation. Don't let anyone shake your confidence with an insincere or "gotcha" question.

Take all questions calmly, listen intently, form a professional response, and share your ideas. That's what you're there for—to share in the best interest of all who are present.

Action Steps

1. Finalize your presentation script and do your dress rehearsal as described earlier in this chapter.
2. In planning for your next presentation, sketch out what your "home base" should look like. What do you need on hand as you're presenting? Plan for it.
3. Practice your paraphrasing and summarizing skills in everyday conversations. Strive to improve your skills.
4. In thinking about your next presentation, what questions might participants have that could be difficult to answer? Play the "devil's advocate," brainstorming a few of these questions. Then draft your answers to them. (This activity will prepare you to handle difficult questions when you must, on the spot and "live" with your audience.)

CHAPTER SIX

Leave 'Em Asking for More

When you give a presentation, you are providing the gift of fresh ideas to your audience. You're asking them to change their practice, and change is extremely difficult. So it only stands to reason that your audience members need additional support after the presentation is over.

Additional support can come in various forms. For example, more personal contact with you, including additional inservice sessions, may be in order. People may find support in using hard-copy and online materials you have provided. They might also want to attend synchronous and asynchronous learning meetings or use technological platforms like Twitter, Facebook, and Ning to continue conversing about the ideas you shared when you were there "live."

Setting Up for the Long Term

Marcia Tate (2004) reminds us to avoid what she calls "pigeon staff development"—someone flies in, drops a load, and flies off (p. xxviii). Tate is not the only staff development expert to say that staff development without follow-up is futile. My colleague (and internationally respected educational researcher) Doug Reeves has documented that it takes seven follow-up days of work to implement what was taught and learned in one day of staff development (http://www.lead andlearn.com/app/webroot/reeves-presentation-downloads/100119-855-WV -Berkeley.pdf).

From large-scale research Reeves and some of my other colleagues have conducted just in the past year, we have also discovered that *poor* implementation of any initiative actually results in worse student achievement results than *no implementation at all* (http://www.leadandlearn.com/app/webroot/reeves-presentation-downloads/100119-855-WV-Berkeley.pdf). Therefore it behooves every presenter to think about the long term while working in the short term.

At a minimum, consider what people need to do *after* you finish speaking. Provide them with examples and suggestions throughout your presentation so that they can envision what will happen next very concretely.

One way to nudge people to envision the actions they must take after an in-service is to use the question stem, "How do you see this working . . . ?" (Knight, 2002, p. 24). This stem asks them to think realistically and to pre-plan for the innovation. It also helps to spin things in a positive manner rather than allowing people to complain.

For example, when I've presented specific, writing-across-the-curriculum strategies, I ask, "How do you see this working with your students?" Then I allow people to pair share or talk at their tables about possible applications.

In these same sessions, I also take questions about potential stumbling blocks or challenges the strategy might present after teachers have had a chance to envision the *successful application* of the strategy. This particular question stem first pushes people to talk about success—the "working" of the strategy—before considering what might not work. That's why this particular stem is so useful—because it focuses on the positive.

If possible, build in short periods of innovation application talk throughout your presentation. Five minutes before the lunch break, you can ask folks to turn to a neighbor or to write silently for two minutes about how they could use the ideas presented thus far.

Throughout the session, use Post-It notes or index cards to have participants jot an application idea or question and hand it in to you so you can address it. Also ask people to think about what they are teaching or what they are doing in their schools in the two or three weeks after your session. Help them immediately apply the ideas you are sharing by having them offer examples of what they could do in thirty days or less. This keeps them focused on the *doing* that must occur after the talking is done.

The Importance of the "Leave-Behind"

You have spent a great deal of time and energy creating an engaging visual and verbal presentation. Both you and the PowerPoint show are critical to the learning of your participants, but there is a third "teacher" to consider as well—the handout.

The hard-copy materials you leave behind with your participants serve as support for them as they begin to implement the changes you have proposed. These materials also serve as potential "reconnectors" that allow audience members to follow up with you for further work.

Remember George Costanza on the show *Seinfeld*? One of his strategies on a date so that the woman would see him again was to do the "leave-behind." He would leave a glove, hat, scarf, or other item behind at the woman's home, thus setting up a second meeting, supposedly just to retrieve the item. But George would leverage that meeting into a second date if possible.

Your handouts serve a similar purpose. If anyone wants to continue the relationship with you, informally or formally (through arranging additional presentations), the handout is the link that remains after the speaking engagement is over.

A professionally created handout is a must. *Never, ever print your slides and use them as your handout.* Yes, PowerPoint software gives you this option—but choose not to take this option! If you have used powerful images for much of your presentation, then why would you print those images on paper? They mean something when the audience is looking at them and listening to your powerful narrative. They mean nothing when printed, miniscule, on a sheet of paper.

One low-stress (for you), high-engagement (for the audience) method for a handout is to engage participants in making their own handout templates during the first few minutes of your presentation. Take this time to show them some note-taking forms that can also be used with students, like Cornell notes and tree charts. Have plenty of notebook paper or plain printer paper on hand, plus pencils, pens, and markers. (See the end of this chapter for examples of these forms.)

Using Technology across Time and Space to Support Ongoing Learning

Webinars and other online meetings can be used for the ongoing learning of the educators to whom you have previously presented. Depending on the online format you use, your attendees may be able to see your face, or they may see only slides or a computer desktop view as they hear your voice (over the Internet or a phone connection).

In such meetings, you can use many of your best presenting skills and connect with the audience best if they can see your face, but even if they can only hear you, you can still do a strong presentation. You must remember to be more exaggerated in all that you do if your audience can't see you. Your slides may have to contain more text so that the audience gets all the critical information they need in this situation, too.

Using blogs, wikis, or other online forums to share ideas after or between presentations is another way to keep your audience members connected and engaged in discussing the innovations that they are attempting. Two of the best online platforms that allow you to control the members of your group and the content of the postings are Ning.com and Wikispaces.com.

Example 1
Cornell Notes
Tehipite Middle School
May 5, 2005
Facilitator: Dr. Angela Peery, Center for Performance Assessment
Classroom Instruction That Works: Review of Book and Instructional Planning for the Present and for the Coming Year
Essential Questions: Which strategies should be applied frequently and consistently to increase student achievement? Why is vocabulary instruction of special importance? How can I use all that I have learned from this book in my instructional planning?

Key Points (Main Ideas)	Details, Connections, Etc.
Most important features to remember of "the essential nine"	
	Note-taking/summarizing Homework Nonlinguistic representations (NLRs)
Using the "essential nine" and other strategies to increase achievement in vocabulary	
Instructional planning template ideas	

Summary of Today's Session:

Example 2
Cornell Notes
Tehipite Middle School
November 4, 2004
Facilitator: Angela Peery, Center for Performance Assessment
Effective Teaching Strategies: Homework and Practice
Essential Questions: What data shows that homework and practice are effective instructional strategies? What must I remember about providing practice and utilizing homework as instructional strategies?

Key Points (Main Ideas)	Details, Connections, Etc.
Research and Theory about Homework: • Purpose • Amount • Parent Involvement Implications for Teaching: • HW Policy • HW Design • Feedback Research and Theory about Practice: • Mastery • Shaping Implications for Teaching: • Accuracy and Speed • Design • Understanding of Processes	
Summary	

Example 3

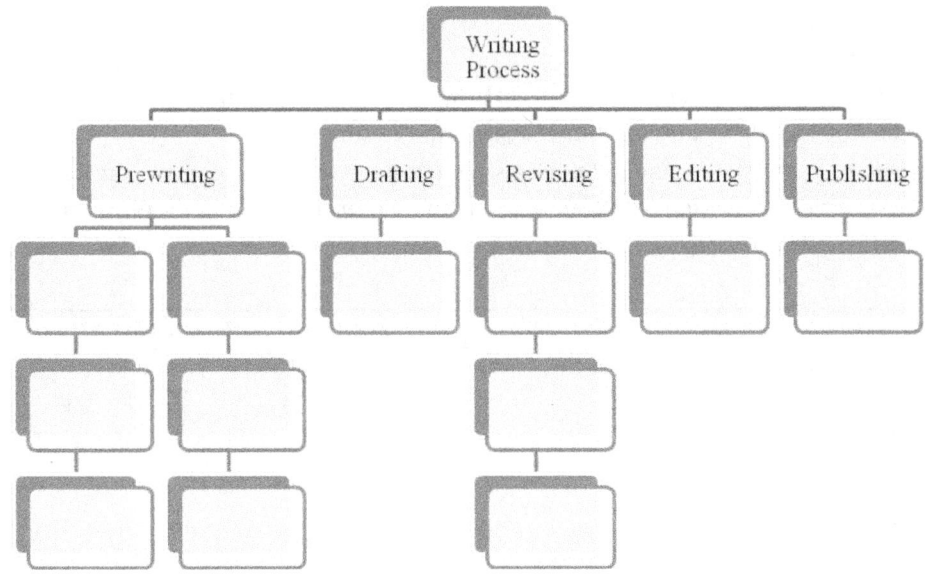

Figure 6.1. Tree Chart Visual

CHAPTER SEVEN

Good Reads

Thank you for reading this book and partnering with me in this journey toward more compelling presentations.

The professional learning of teachers is of critical importance as students worldwide are held accountable for meeting higher academic standards than ever before. Staff developers like you, who facilitate the professional learning of other educators, have to make every minute count, and enhancing your presentation design and delivery skills will help you do just that.

However, your time for reading and reflection is limited. So while I hope that this book has been a worthwhile read for you, I'd like to recommend other resources to inspire you further. The rest of this chapter will take the form of an annotated bibliography, with the resources listed in alphabetical order by the primary author's name.

Books

Altman, Rick. 2007. *Why Most PowerPoint Presentations Suck and How You Can Make Them Better* (1st edition). Pleasanton, CA: Harvest Books.

This book is written in a conversational style and includes tons of technical tips, some much easier to learn than others. The book is not a visual delight, like Duarte's and Reynolds' books are. It's much more like a manual. It's a good read after you've schooled yourself in the work of Duarte and Reynolds—certainly not before, unless you're so techno-savvy that you want to dig right into the software and try things you've never tried before. For the "big view," I still recommend Duarte and Reynolds ahead of Altman.

Atkinson, Cliff. 2008. *Beyond Bullet Points: Using Microsoft Office PowerPoint 2007 to Create Presentations That Inform, Motivate, and Inspire.* Redmond, WA: Microsoft Press.

This book takes a very linear (yet entertaining) approach to designing presentations. The early sections on communication and the explanation of narrative structure are well done and help you distinguish the forest from the trees.

Atkinson helps you articulate your ideas, ground them in elements of storytelling, and put the technology to work—in that order. Again, I recommend this book as a good read after reading either Duarte or Reynolds (or both).

Duarte, Nancy. 2008. *Slideology: The Art and Science of Creating Great Presentations.* Sebastopol, CA: O'Reilly Media, Inc.

Nancy Duarte is the person who heads up the design firm behind Al Gore's film *An Inconvenient Truth*, which was the first PowerPoint presentation to win an Academy Award. That fact alone was enough to entice me to buy the book.

This book is more technical than *Presentation Zen* and is therefore a great choice for following up on the ideas presented there and applying them to slide show design.

Chapter 7 on the use of visual elements is an excellent primer that should be studied by every person who uses PowerPoint as a teaching tool. It contains lessons in choosing backgrounds, colors, text, and images. This particular chapter reminded me of some basic art principles (like creating a color palette that works based on the properties of the color wheel) in ways that finally stuck with me like never before, regardless of the training sessions I've had in both art and technology over the span of my twenty-four-year education career.

Chapter 3, Creating Diagrams, and chapter 4, Displaying Data, should be required reading for every person who presents at national education conferences and every speaker who must address a school board. Instructors at both the undergraduate and graduate school levels should study these two chapters as well.

Chapters 3 through 8 are actually a short course in graphic design as applied to PowerPoint and would serve most staff developers well, even if they never read another thing about design. These chapters are comprehensive and easy to digest.

Case studies are used throughout the book to illustrate good design, unified core messages, and excellence in delivery. Duarte also graciously shares a great deal of her own creative process, including original sketches.

Godin, Seth. *Really Bad PowerPoint.* An e-book pdf is available online at http://www.sethgodin.com/freeprize/reallybad-1.pdf. For an HTML version see http://sethgodin.typepad.com/seths_blog/2007/01/really_bad_powe.html.

This short book (a booklet, really) is hilarious. Read it and share it!

Heath, Chip, and Dan Heath. 2007. *Made to Stick: Why Some Ideas Survive and Others Die.* New York: Random House.

The Heath brothers lay out the six core principles of "sticky" messages—those stories or ideas that take hold. The six key principles are simplicity, unexpectedness, concreteness, credibility, emotions, and stories.

Garr Reynolds builds his early chapters of *Presentation Zen* on these principles and summarizes them nicely, so read this book only if you want to delve deeper. It's a light, easy, and fun read and should be part of your library if you are interested in powerful storytelling in general.

Reynolds, Garr. 2008. *Presentation Zen: Simple Ideas on Presentation Design and Delivery*. Berkeley, CA: New Riders Press.

This is the book that started my obsession. First, it's a beautifully designed book; it's just one of those books you want to hold, touch, admire, and urge other people to buy. A Zen aesthetic is visible throughout.

Second, it's a fast read. The tone is engaging and the ideas compelling yet simply stated.

Reynolds lays the groundwork early: most PowerPoint presentations are done poorly; our high-touch, conceptual age now requires a different, more emotional kind of communication; we must change our lazy, bad PowerPoint habits.

Reynolds advocates "planning analog," using basic tools like pencil, paper, Post-It notes, white boards, and markers to draft ideas long before turning to PowerPoint to begin to design slides. He includes many helpful sidebars throughout the books, including articles written by Nancy Duarte, Seth Godin, and Guy Kawasaki. Abundant examples of well-designed slides appear, as do examples of slide "makeovers." He teaches basic design lessons like using empty space well, using grids to hold designs, directing the eye with images, and using contrast without being overly technical.

This book is simply a must-read for anyone wanting to improve his or her presentation skills. It's a great companion to Nancy Duarte's book *Slideology*. The two can be read as a pair within a short time frame and give even the experienced presenter much to contemplate.

Weissman, Jerry. 2009. *Presenting to Win: The Art of Telling Your Story, Updated and Expanded Edition*. Upper Saddle River, NJ: Pearson Education.

This book is all about presenting. Weissman is a famous and very experienced presenter and presentation coach. His book includes sections on identifying your real goals and sharpening your message, staying focused on what your audience really wants, capturing and holding your audience's attention, and crafting the power presentation.

If you want to become a better presenter, this book should be on your shelf. You will go back to it again and again.

Williams, Robin. 2008. *The Non-Designer's Design Book* (3rd edition). Berkeley, CA: Peachpit Press.

This book is lovely—the pages are laid out beautifully, the paper is slick, and the colors and typefaces are striking. Williams teaches some basic publishing and graphic design information in a witty, readable style.

If you buy no other book on general design (mainly of print materials), *buy this one*. The lessons are timeless, and you'll never look at a brochure, sign, menu, or business card in quite the same way again.

Websites, Blogs, and Other Resources

All the sites recommended here were functional as this book went to press.

I highly recommend Nancy Duarte's blog at http://blog.duarte.com. Some especially helpful articles include "Five Simple Tweaks" at http://blog.duarte.com/2009/02/lessons-from-ted-5-simple-tweaks, "Cliché of the Week: Clip Art" at http://blog.duarte.com/2008/11/cliche-of-the-week-clip-art, and "The Trouble with Transitions" series (episode 1) available at http://blog.duarte.com/2008/10/the-trouble-with-transitions-episode-1.

Garr Reynolds' Presentation Tips at http://www.garrreynolds.com/Presentation/index.html are also very useful. Reynolds has a blog at http://www.presentationzen.com. One of his most interesting entries is "Make Your Next Presentation Naked" at http://presentationzen.blogs.com/presentationzen/2005/10/make_your_next_.html.

Rick Altman's site on better presenting and better PowerPoint can be found at http://www.betterppt.com.

Executive presentation coach Jerry Weissman's blog is at http://powerltd.com/category/blogs.

Seth Godin's blog at http://sethgodin.typepad.com always has provocative articles about presenting, sales, marketing, and work, in general. You can sign up to receive his posts via e-mail. Many of them are provocative enough to share—across many types of organizations and work situations.

In chapter 4, I discussed the importance of correct, deep breathing. See the article at http://health.discovery.com/centers/althealth/deepbreath/deepbreathe.html for more information.

References

Altman, Rick. 2007. *Why Most PowerPoint Presentations Suck and How You Can Make Them Better* (1st edition). Pleasanton, CA: Harvest Books.

Atkinson, Cliff. 2008. *Beyond Bullet Points: Using Microsoft Office PowerPoint 2007 to Create Presentations That Inform, Motivate, and Inspire.* Redmond, WA: Microsoft Press.

Duarte, Nancy. 2008. *Slideology: The Art and Science of Creating Great Presentations.* Sebastopol, CA: O'Reilly Media, Inc.

Engaging Classroom Assessments Seminar. 2009. The Leadership and Learning Center.

Garmston, Robert. 2006. "Skillful Paraphrasing Allows Groups to Examine What Is Being Said." *Journal of Staff Development* 27, no. 3: 65–66.

Godin, Seth. 2001. *Really Bad PowerPoint.* E-book available online at http://www.sethgodin.com/freeprize/reallybad-1.pdf and http://sethgodin.typepad.com/seths_blog/2007/01/really_bad_powe.html.

Heath, Chip, and Dan Heath. 2007. *Made to Stick: Why Some Ideas Survive and Others Die.* New York: Random House.

Koegel, Timothy. 2002. *The Exceptional Presenter: A Proven Formula to Open Up! And Own the Room.* Austin, TX: Greenleaf Book Group Press.

Knight, Jim. 2002. *Partnership Learning Fieldbook.* Lawrence: University of Kansas Center for Research on Learning.

Kosslyn, S. M. 2007. *Clear and to the Point: Eight Psychological Principles for Compelling PowerPoint Presentations.* New York: Oxford University Press.

Lee, Harper. 1960. *To Kill a Mockingbird.* Philadelphia: Lippincott.

Margolis, Jason. 2009. "How Teachers Lead Teachers." *Educational Leadership* 66, no. 5. Available at http://www.ascd.org/publications/educational_leadership/feb09/vol66/num05/How_Teachers_Lead_Teachers.aspx.

Merriam Webster Online Dictionary. 2009. Available at http://www.merriam-webster.com.

MetLife Survey of the American Teacher. 2008. Available at http://www.eric.ed.gov/ERICDocs/data/ericdocs2sql/content_storage_01/0000019b/80/43/68/44.pdf.

Pink, Dan. 2006. *A Whole New Mind: Why Right-Brainers Will Rule the Future*. New York: Berkley Publishing Group.

Reeves, Douglas. 2009. Presentation. Available at http://www.leadandlearn.com/app/webroot/reeves-presentation-downloads/100119-855-WV-Berkeley.pdf.

Reynolds, Garr. 2005. http://www.garrreynolds.com/Presentation/delivery.html.

Reynolds, Garr. 2008. *Presentation Zen: Simple Ideas on Presentation Design and Delivery*. Berkeley, CA: New Riders Press.

Tate, Marcia. 2004. *Sit and Get Won't Grow Dendrites: 20 Professional Learning Strategies That Engage the Adult Brain*. Thousand Oaks, CA: Corwin Press.

Weissman, Jerry. 2009. *Presenting to Win: The Art of Telling Your Story, Updated and Expanded Edition*. Upper Saddle River, NJ: Pearson Education.

Williams, Robin. 2008. *The Non-Designer's Design Book* (3rd edition). Berkeley, CA: Peachpit Press.

www.ingramcontent.com/pod-product-compliance
Lightning Source LLC
Chambersburg PA
CBHW080739230426
43665CB00020B/2792